MidLife Mojo

12 Easy Ways to Maintain Your Healthy MidLife Weight

STRESS
FADS
$$$$$

Wendy Trevarthen

First published in 2018.
2nd Edition published by Ultimate World Publishing 2024.
Copyright © 2024 Wendy Trevarthen

ISBN

Paperback: 978-1-925830-25-5
Ebook: 978-1-925830-46-0

Wendy Trevarthen has asserted her rights under the Copyright, Designs and Patents Act 1988 to be identified as the author of this work. The information in this book is based on the author's experiences and opinions. The publisher specifically disclaims responsibility for any adverse consequences which may result from use of the information contained herein. Permission to use information has been sought by the author. Any breaches will be rectified in further editions of the book.

All rights reserved. No part of this publication may be reproduced, stored in or introduced into a retrieval system, or transmitted in any form, or by any means (electronic, mechanical, photocopying, recording or otherwise) without the prior written permission of the author. Any person who does any unauthorised act in relation to this publication may be liable to criminal prosecution and civil claims for damages. Enquiries should be made through the publisher.

Cover design: Ultimate World Publishing
Layout and typesetting: Ultimate World Publishing

Ultimate World Publishing
Diamond Creek,
Victoria Australia 3089
www.writeabook.com.au

I have recently been working to achieve better control of a skin condition through a healthier diet, focussed towards whole foods. After learning Wendy had a long background in the medical field and the fact that we seemed a good fit to work together, I decided to work with Wendy as a coach for my personal challenge.

Wendy was genuinely compassionate and empathetic when my description of working on my challenge brought me to tears. Her delivery and style are honest and straightforward without being pushy or demanding.

My experience working with Wendy was extremely pleasurable. My skin condition is showing a major and much-needed improvement. Wendy made sure I had a plan in place for me to take continued action over the next few months upon exit of our coaching agreement. I would highly recommend Wendy for any health goal-related coaching for which you might have need, be it physical or mental. Wendy offers great results at very reasonable prices for the services rendered. Thank you, Wendy!

Leigh Scheidell
Video Creative

Testimonials

I stopped doing the outdoor activities I loved and looking after my health when my boys were born, because I thought I was just too busy with them and work. It became a continuous, vicious circle, week after week.

By the weekend, I was tired, and trying to play catch up on things I hadn't completed while pigging out on unhealthy food. I kept thinking I didn't have time to do the things I loved. I was just existing, going through the motions and wondering – was this it? There must be more to life. Enough was enough!

With Wendy's help, I started focussing on the important aspects of my health and wellbeing. I got back to doing things I love; my energy levels are increasing, and my weight is down. I am working on improving little by little each week and realise it will be an ongoing process.

Wendy makes sense and makes it easy!
   Tania Potgeiter
   CSO at MarkTwo Consulting

Dedication

To my wonderful parents for instilling in me the core value of 'family first'. Dad, who showed me through his own resilience that you can conquer anything in life and learn to appreciate every day as a gift. Mum, for your tenacious Scottish spirit, which is now in my genetic makeup.

Dad: 'As long as you know you have given 100%, you can't go wrong.'

For my loving partner Nigel, who has supported me through my own transformation, and to my two adult children, Rhiannon and William, who have lived my journey without asking too many questions.

For little Emma and Chloe, the surprise packet that came when no one was looking. Two stars that shine bright every day, to allow me to be the Nifty Nannie at Fifty that I have always strived to be.

Contents

Introduction	i
1. Your Key Motivators	1
2. It's Not All About the Weight	9
3. Unlock Your Happiness Toolbox	17
4. Bust Your Midlife Clutter	25
5. Diet Is A Dirty Word	33
6. Your Movement Mojo	47
7. Aging with Dignity	59
8. Thrive Despite Chronic Conditions	69
9. Managing the Mother Juggle	79
10. Career Crossroads	89
11. Avoiding the Financial Vacuum	97
12. You Did It!	103
About the Author	109
Speaker Profile	111
Packages	115

Introduction

The inspiration for this book

The idea for writing this book came to me over the last four or five years. I have been working in nursing for a long time, and I see many people who have made questionable health decisions for their lives, resulting in complications of having one or many illnesses.

When I was clinically obese in my forties, I knew that if I didn't do something about my own health I would be end up being the kind of statistic that I was nursing.

This book is primarily for women who are overwhelmed in these middle years, when they're bound by their own family responsibilities, responsibility for their elderly parents, for their work commitments, and at times overwhelmed with themselves.

Throughout my transformation in my forties, I had to deal with issues such as self-confidence and self-image, and after recognising this, I just wanted to regain a sense of control over my weight. With my nursing background I knew what I had to do to change, but I had developed so many unhealthy habits that breaking them meant I had to reset my attitude towards myself.

What I learned through those years about myself parallels many others' experiences, and I feel drawn to pass on my learnings to enable others to reflect and make healthier lifestyle choices. Having a support crew, a coach, and clearer, accurate information and education about those choices is vital for success.

I did want to convey my own exploration of the common misconceptions that are out there to make it easier for others, and particularly women, to navigate their way towards healthier and happier versions of themselves. It is only through making better decisions through all aspects of our health that we can have any chance of fighting the obesity epidemic all around us, and to avoid becoming another statistic.

Free government programs are available, but I have found that they are centred on a medical screening model, and there is very little available for those who want to take control over their own destiny at a time and a place that suits their life commitments and circumstances.

This book can be used as a reference; it can be a guide for ideas that you might like to adapt into your own life. There are tips and insights into the backbone of wellness concepts. There is the key message of simplicity, at a low cost, with a 'no fad' approach to lifestyle strategies.

I believe this age is a chance to take stock, reflect and invest in what your next fifty years is going to look like.

Introduction

The inspiration for my work

The inspiration for what I currently do came from my dad's story.

When I was seventeen, my father developed a disease called Guillain-Barré Syndrome. He was struck down suddenly, becoming a quadriplegic. He was in ICU and ventilated within hours of developing his first symptoms. He slowly regained some movement and spent a considerable amount of time in physical rehabilitation.

When he came home, some two-and-a-half years later, my mum looked after him for the final six years of his life. During that time, my mum had to relocate to a home to accommodate Dad's needs, retire from work, and source another income stream to enable them to live, as a fulltime care facility was not an option. He was fifty-seven when he passed away from complications. I was twenty-five, with a new baby.

That experience not only inspired me to become a nurse, but it also instilled in me the value of each day that we have. As a result, I pursued a nursing career and out of that experience, I learned to look at the patient or client as family, adapting my approach to them and their relatives to support them within the context of their circumstances.

Every day is a blessing. Having undergone my own transformation during my forties, and with my own children and grandchildren at this stage in my life, I feel compelled to put my experience out there, and to create a sense of purpose from that life experience. My own transformation resulted from me recognising how precious my life is, and it is this purpose that I have used as the backbone of my career.

The only limit to the height of your achievement is the reach of your dreams, and your willingness to work hard to achieve them.
Michelle Obama

1. Your Key Motivators

Don't wait for a light at the end of the tunnel, stride down there and light the bloody thing yourself.
Sara Jane Henderson

YOU ARE UNIQUE. There is no one on this planet like you. You are an imperfect, perfect, human specimen. Your needs and wants are unique to you and nobody else. Your desire to be the best version of yourself and your journey towards that goal is unique to you. The challenges we face in our midlife years are numerous and the navigation of these is achievable if you have the right attitude and motivation.

Firstly, ask yourself, why are you on this journey?

During this chapter, we will explore your journey and unpack it, so that you have your own, unique reason why you are going down this path.

We are going to uncover what actually drives you forward and the consequences of your choices, and in doing so, we're going to explore your mind-set and your attitude towards making the change for yourself. Ultimately, you will understand yourself a lot better.

When I started my health journey in my mid-forties, I had no idea that I had a problem. I was in complete denial. I remember the exact day and the scenario that made all the difference and it hit me like an anvil.

I was working as a unit manager in a major north Queensland public hospital, and I had to urgently walk rather briskly from one end of the corridor to the other, and then quickly go up three flights of stairs. When I got to the top of the stairs, I was completely out of breath. What was wrong with me? I was playing three games of netball, I was eating what I thought was a reasonable diet, I had a lot of things going on in my personal life that I thought I was keeping in balance, but I could not believe how out of breath I was at the top of those stairs.

A few years later after I made some drastic changes, I looked back at that time and I tried to find some photos of myself then, and lo and behold, I had gone through a period of my life where I had not taken any photos of myself. Looking back on it, I realised that I was quite ashamed of how I looked.

The house we owned at the time only had mirrors showing your reflection from the waist up, so although I was quite aware that I was a little bit overweight, I did not realise the extent of my obesity. I was so consumed with everything else going on in my life; I was busy just trying to keep everything else on track.

I was determined to keep everything ticking over, to keep the household running, to keep my children healthy and happy (which I think I successfully achieved), but I had totally neglected myself. I was all too consumed in the day-to-day activities of going to work, keeping the household going, and maintaining the children's activities, that I had avoided seeing how much of an impact this had on my weight.

Something had to change, and I made the decision at the top of those stairs to make conscious choices: about my health and fitness, about my emotional wellbeing, about my work-life balance. I subsequently implemented these choices, resulting in a dramatic change in my attitude and the resultant weight loss.

I had become an obesity statistic, and I was ashamed. Sometimes you need an anvil to get you going. A scare; a realisation that you are mortal.

Sixty-three percent of Australian adults are above the healthy weight range.[1]

Sometimes making the change can be frightening. You feel like you are constantly challenging yourself. You're looking at ways to improve your situation, and sometimes change can be daunting. Fear is one of the main reasons why we elect not to make those changes. We're happy in our comfort zones, we're happy with the way things are, because they're running along smoothly.

Over the years I've found that if you don't challenge yourself and your boundaries, they're never going to move. It's never going to make a difference for you.

---

1. Australian Institute of Health and Welfare, 2016. 'Healthy Communities: Overweight and obesity rates across Australia, 2014–15', viewed September 2018, <https://www.myhealthycommunities.gov.au/our-reports/overweight-and-obesity-rates/december-2016>.

Sometimes we are blind, thinking that staying the same is beneficial to us. If we can identify why staying the same can be detrimental to our long-term health, then we can really be true to ourselves and see the consequences. Where you are now may not be where you want to be in another five to ten years' time.

Therefore, we need to look at the reasons why we want to change. They could be obvious to you, but sometimes they are not. Listening to professional advice or the well-intentioned comment from a close friend or relative – or indeed having an anvil moment like mine – may be the lightbulb moment that you need.

Our lives are so busy that it's important to take time to reflect on where you're going and where you want to be.

If you don't make some of the changes in your life, where are you going to be? What are you going to look like in five to ten years' time? What are you going to *feel* like in five to ten years' time? What are some of the things that you can or cannot do in five to ten years' time, if you don't make the changes?

Once you've identified where you want to be, what are some of the things that are stopping you from getting there? There are obvious things, like time, your own motivation, change in a diet, change in an exercise routine or even starting any of those activities. Where do you start? Are your family, your environment or your workplace supportive of the steps that you want to take? What drives you to seek better solutions to enable you to make the changes? What gives you the drive to push past any barriers?

For me in my stair scenario, I could immediately see that if I stayed on the same path, I would quickly become one of the patients that I was looking after at the time. That was the anvil that hit me. I did not want to end up being like that: I wanted to avoid chronic illness later in life. I wanted to see myself in my eighties enjoying time with people that I loved and being an active person in my relationships and my community.

What would it look like for you? What do you see as your key drivers in moving you forward? Is it the people in your life, in your family, in your work life? Do you have life goals that you want to achieve?

How important are those life goals to you?

Find your five

The well-known philosopher Jim Rohn advocates that you need to find your five key people to help you stay focussed on your true purpose. I challenge you to use this advice. These five supports do not need to be in your immediate circle. They could include a literature hero, or a personal development guru that you feel connected to. They could be on a video platform, via a podcast, or in films or TV. These are the people that you turn to for their honest opinion of how you are going, who will find the words you need to hear to start your journey, move to the next step, to motivate you to try harder, or to keep you on track.

Confronting fear

I know that you're scared of making the changes, I can hear you saying to yourself that you don't really know whether you will be successful. You're doubting yourself, limiting yourself to what you can achieve. Think back on a time when you had a sports coach encouraging you to push further, reach further, go over that line, and extend yourself. Alternatively, think back to when you were limited for time when writing an essay and you knew that you had to get it completed. And you did it.

We're always talking about giving 110% of ourselves to our goals. What is it that gets you over that line and pushes you? Is it a time factor? Is it someone that you're letting down, that you would want to please to complete that task?

What I want you to consider doing is to internalise that motivation, whatever it is. Use it to motivate you to drive yourself forward. Think about the reasons why you're on this journey and use that as a carrot in front of you to push you forward and get you going.

Sometimes the challenges that you face seem a bit overwhelming, and it's all too hard. I suggest you use this book to break those things down. The following eleven chapters contain strategies you can employ to break that overwhelming goal down into chunk-sized pieces.

Maybe you've tried something like this in the past, and hey, arriving at our midlife, haven't we tried it all? Maybe it is a process of taking three steps forwards and two steps backwards, but I tell you what, you'll be a single step further ahead. The important thing is to recognise what pulled you back. Reflect on that and use that to move you forward.

Actively ask for feedback; sometimes we do not recognise what the block is. Oh yes, I hear you – it is easier said than done. But if you're moving forward each time that it happens, then you're further ahead than when you started.

Developing a deep, emotional attachment to your drivers to help you to move forward can really connect you with the goal that you've set for yourself.

Visualising your motivators

Using imagery, pictures, photographs, key diagrams and keeping them handy on a wall or in your diary can motivate you to move yourself forward every day.

Keeping an image on your smart phone that you know represents what you've just unpacked, can be an easy way of reminding yourself why you're on this journey.

Don't forget to celebrate. If you've broken all of these goals down into bite-sized pieces, when you get to the end of one of your bite-sized pieces, celebrate. Give yourself a pat on the back, look for appraisal from those that are around you and if they willingly give you that praise, accept it with grace and honour. Avoid celebrating the old-fashioned way, by choosing unhealthy options.

Instead, find other healthier ways to help you celebrate your achievements. It could be a trip away; it could be simply walking around the block with music in your ears, feeling happy and proud of yourself. Whatever way incorporates a healthier lifestyle, use it to help you celebrate.

> **Healthy options to take:**
> 1. Understand what motivates you at a deep emotional level.
> 2. Confront fear and push forward.
> 3. Develop some visual reminders of your motivators and have them near you.
> 4. Celebrate healthily.

Now that you have found your key motivators, let's use them throughout the rest of this book and tackle exactly what you would like to change.

What is the most rigorous of law of our being? Growth. No smallest atom or our moral, or physical structure can stand still a year. It grows – it must grow; nothing can prevent it.
Mark Twain

2. It's Not All About the Weight

If you don't know where you are going, any road will get you there.
Lewis Carroll

WHEN DECIDING EXACTLY WHAT to focus on for improving your overall health and wellness, sometimes the underlying root of the problem is difficult to pinpoint. It can involve one or many aspects of your wellbeing. Often invisible interruptions can camouflage the obvious solutions to making healthier choices and developing better routines.

Sometimes the questions are complicated, and the answers are simple.
Dr Seuss

During this chapter, we'll cover various aspects of your health and wellness.

Working through an activity may trigger some points of concern or underlying aspects of your wellness that you may not have previously considered, and which might impact on your wellbeing. By the end of this chapter, you may have more of an insight into the contributing factors that may be blocking your ability to maintain your healthy weight. By being aware of and then addressing some of those other issues, you might take the focus off your weight and enjoy improving those areas of your development that enable you to feel more fulfilled in your life more generally. Maintaining your weight will then become easier.

You'll understand the impact of those issues and see a change of attitude towards all aspects of your life, which will in turn be of benefit. You'll rid yourself of any guilt or past dilemmas you've had dealing with these aspects of your wellness. This will add to your confidence in being able to challenge yourself and move forward in managing them. You will gain momentum in controlling those underlying factors and move onwards to the next one as a healthier routine becomes a habit.

A positive outcome from this is that people around you will notice a difference in you immediately. Simply looking at these things gives you a sense of control over what's happening within you, and that sense of control can be felt by the people in your life. What we're trying to eliminate here are the underlying reasons stopping you from taking charge over your health and wellness – or to minimise the effects that they have on you.

Aspects of your wellness to consider

Let's take a few moments to consider some of the aspects of your wellness. You will notice that none of them specifically involves nutrition and exercise. These are bundled up into one heading of *Health & Fitness*. The activity requires you to rate how fulfilled you think you are in those areas, with a score out of ten (ten meaning that you are totally fulfilled). Let's examine all of these.

Close relationships such as friends and family
Some people say you can pick your friends, but you cannot pick your family. These days we have so many different varieties of families, and a lot of broken households that live under separate roofs. Alongside that comes the other aspects of your environment: the food that you eat, the exercise that you partake in each day. Whether we realise it or not, we are influenced greatly by the people that we spend the most time with.

Take a moment to think about that.

Surrounding yourself with positive people is easier said than done, and probably needs to happen over an extended period. In order for the people dear to you to support you in what you're trying to achieve, you need to have open communication for those relationships to function.

Your personal growth and development
How do we improve relationships with family and friends to enable them to have positive benefits for you? Improvement comes through various aspects of your own personal growth and your own development, your consciousness and awareness of how you relate to other people and how other people relate to you. There is a plethora of personal growth and development books and resources out there. I truly believe that most people understand where they're sitting

with their own development, and what skills and knowledge they need to develop for them to have positive relationships around them. We can always improve.

I encourage you to actively seek out those resources to improve on your own capacity to deal with the relationships around you. Develop a habit of reading or watching something in the personal growth and development literature for ten minutes every day and watch as your self-confidence and self-esteem improve over time.

Spirituality
Spirituality means different things to different people. When you first saw the heading, what thoughts came into your mind? What did spirituality mean to you? Write it down.

If it was foremost in your mind when you read the heading, it's of great importance to you. Your own gauge of spirituality is your own gauge and again, the impact of family and friends may have an impact on your score here. However, what I want you to do is to think about how important it is to you.

Finances
In this day of commercialism and materialism, you might rate finances at a high level of importance or it may rate extremely low – again it's extremely personal. Unfortunately, if our finances don't match our lifestyle then there is a huge imbalance that can lead to implications for our health and wellness.

Career and purpose
Do your career and business goals match the motivations that you identified in chapter one? Do they rate at a higher level for you? Have you achieved, or are you achieving, the goals that you had set for yourself?

2. It's Not All About the Weight

What you'll find with your career and business is that it may change over your life span, but this gauge is where you are at the moment.

I'll give you an example from my own experience. During the time that I gained a lot of weight, my attitude was that I wanted to be quite successful in my nursing career, and I believed I was. However, gaining success during that time was detrimental to my home-life balance, as I put a lot of time and effort into gaining the qualifications and moving forward in my nursing career.

Do I regret what I did? Not at all. It gave me the experience, skills and knowledge to fulfil the position requirements at the time. But looking back on it, I wonder if I could have made some better choices regarding my family commitments.

Romantic partner
How fulfilled do you feel in this area? The person that we spend the most time with is usually our partner. It's the person that you confide in, it's the person that you live life with; it's the person who is your best friend, your beau, the person that you want to lean on.

And if you're single, and happy with the single life, you could rate that quite highly. Consider a close friend or a relation that you hold dear, rate your experience with them.

Play
They say we're all big kids at heart. Are you enjoying being an adult kid or is it an aspect of your life that you want to improve on? For some silly reason, adults have lost the ability to smile and laugh at themselves. They sometimes feel a bit embarrassed or ashamed when they break out in roaring laughter or do something silly. We know how important having fun is for our health, so happiness will be covered in chapter three.

Are you achieving all the recreational activities that you want to achieve, or do you have some bigger goals that you want to tick off?

Giving to others
Again, this is a personal choice. Some people are more giving or show gratitude better than others. Some people make it a lifetime achievement – they want to contribute, give to some cause, or find some way of giving back to the community.

If this is important to you and you feel fulfilled, score that highly. If it's an area that you want to improve, then score it lower accordingly.

Health and fitness
Rate your level of fitness overall. Again, this is a personal gauge of where you want to be, so if your health and fitness is satisfactory for where you want to be and for achieving your goals at this point, then rate that nine or ten out of ten. If it's one area that you want to improve, and see yourself having the capacity to do so, then rate yourself low.

Your environment
Is your physical environment the way that you want it to be? Does it give you the space that you need to be yourself, that allows you to be happy and fulfilled? Does it motivate and lift you? Does it give you a sense of 'you'? Rate this feeling out of ten.

> Knowing what you cannot do is more important
> than knowing what you can.
> **Lucille Ball**

Putting it all together

You can see from your numbers how well you are doing in some areas, and how there are some areas that need improvement. This gives you an idea of what to focus on. If you can identify the top two or three issues to address, you can start to see how you can put them into an action plan. Some of the areas that you've selected will be covered in this book to help you move forward.

One of the key things that needs overcoming is your attitude towards some of your priorities. Recognise that you scored some things so low that it probably is a bit of a challenge for you to move forward. However, if you break them down into small steps and achieve them over a period of time, then the reality is you can't help but move forward.

During my weight loss journey in my forties, and more recently maintaining a healthy weight during midlife, I know that my attitude and the actions I take consistently have led me to success so far, and will move me through my latter years.

Once you've completed this activity, share it with your significant other. Let them give you an honest opinion and tell you whether your interpretation of where you are and where they think you are is one and the same.

As you can see, this chapter has been about recognising those aspects of your wellness that provide the background to why you might be challenged to maintain a healthy weight. Staying consistent is key, and it is okay to slip back occasionally, but what is beneficial to you is to look how far you've come already. Identify how far you've come even since the beginning of this book: you're now into chapter two and you've made a start. Congratulations!

> **Healthy options to take:**
> 1. Look at aspects of your wellness and score your health and wellness on a scale of zero to ten.
> 2. Select two or three aspects of your health and wellness that you want to improve.
> 3. Enlist a significant other to support you on your journey.
> 4. Develop an attitude that's going to be easy rather than hard, by breaking the changes down into small actions.

Yes, you can have it all, but not all at the same time. Set your own priorities, trust your gut and follow your heart.
Quentin Bryce

3. Unlock Your Happiness Toolbox

Happiness is not something that you postpone for the future; it is something that you design for the present.
Jim Rohn

HAPPY PEOPLE LIVE LONGER; it's true. It takes less energy to be happy than to be otherwise, and the effect on the body can be transformational.

Just think back to your childhood. For most people everything was carefree – you could run, play and do what you wanted. How happy most of us were! For some reason as we get older, we lose the fun in our lives and take everything a little bit too seriously.

A happy person speaks not only with their facial expressions, but also with their body language. Very open, clear, bright eyes – they just convey the picture of happiness. The first thing that a baby does when they start using their facial expressions is to smile at someone; it is a genuine expression that they give to everyone.

During this chapter, we'll find that happy place to use as a strategy to help you move forward. You'll feel calmer, and you'll gain a sense of control over who you are. It will help you to think clearly, sleep better and generally help you to cope better with life's challenges.

A study in England followed participants aged between 52 and 79 years of age over a 5-year period. It found that there is positive correlation between how happy they felt and their longevity.[2]

I can hear what you're saying: you feel that your emotions often take over. Being aware of your emotions and having insight into them is key. I always think back to a time in my life when I was extremely stressed. I now know that during that time, the stress I was under contributed to me putting on all the weight that I did in my late thirties.

However, in my late teenage years, through my father's experience, I learned the art of resilience. I learned the value of treating every day as a blessing, and that every day should have happy moments in it. It is a waste of energy and time if you mainly focus on the negative things, especially if they are beyond your control.

In order to understand how all these compounding stresses can impact on your life and ability to feel inner contentment and happiness, it's really important to understand stress and its effect in your body.

---

[2]. Mandal, A, 2011, 'Happiness good for health', *Medical Life Sciences*, viewed September 2018, <https://www.news-medical.net/news/20111101/Happiness-good-for-health-Study.aspx>.

The stress response – how it works

Your nervous system is made up of two components, the central nervous system and the peripheral nervous system (PNS). The PNS is further divided into two, the somatic and the autonomic nervous system (ANS). The ANS is the part that is heavily involved in the stress response. This is the nervous control of any subconscious bodily processes, such as breathing, digestion, reflexes and organ function. This is then divided into two more sub-branches, the sympathetic (fright, fight or flight) and the parasympathetic (rest, digest, and restore). Imbalances between the two can occur instantly, or from compounding imbalances (often, daily stresses that accumulate over time). Both play an important role.

The sympathetic response has worked for us over thousands of years. It has ensured the survival of our species. If we're confronted with a life-threatening situation, the sympathetic nervous system redirects blood flow from our immune and digestive systems to the periphery that is our arms and legs, to enable us to fight or flee. A shadow of this is also achieved by chronic stress, by everyday stresses such as financial worries, the daily grind that you 'put up with', and unhealthy lifestyle choices. These add up over time and shift your body's balance to a drained sympathetic nervous system state.

The parasympathetic response has also worked for us during our evolution. Without it, we would not restore and grow. When we are in our safe, relaxed place, our bodies have the capacity to recover and restore. However, prolonged engagement in the sympathetic state outside your safe place, for example, your comfort zone, results in lethargy, malaise or lacking that 'spring in your step'.

Let's make it real.

In order for you to have balance, you need to aim to equalise your body's exposure to both states. That is mostly within your control.

We live in a busy, busy world... Or do we?

Do we make it busier than it has to be? Or do we have the capacity to slow things down and take things as they come, so that we can expend energy or stimulate our parasympathetic response at times that suit us? With technology changing at an exponential rate, it's vital that we take a step back and use technology to our advantage rather than let it rule our world. We need to allow our environment to give us more time for our parasympathetic responses to rest and restore our bodies.

Buzzword – 'mindfulness'

One of the key strategies that's commonly used is called mindfulness. This is where you can take yourself consciously to a place where you know you can instil a calm aura about yourself. This calm place can be unique to you. Think about a time, a place, or a process where you've felt quite at rest with the world, where you've mindlessly gone off on a creative tangent and allowed yourself to think, feel and smell all the things around you through all five senses. So much so, that you've become totally distracted from the rest of the world.

Some activities that involve doing this include reading a book or enjoying a scenic view like walking through botanic gardens. For some, it might be an exercise activity where you're mindlessly absorbed in what you're doing, such as jogging, swimming, or cycling. It's a place where time goes by and you have no awareness of it. You're in touch with all of your senses and everything is just free. Meditation, yoga and a lot of the martial arts, such as tai chi, all involve an element of mindfulness.

Being aware of stressful situations is also a way of making sure that you know what effect it is having in your body.

Sometimes those close to you may bring that to your attention, and your initial reaction may be that you're in denial, trying to push those suggestions or comments away. But by being open and receptive to those comments, they may be giving you a bit of advice that you probably need to pay attention to.

Keep a journal and write these situations down. It doesn't mean that you must act on them straight away. Just being aware of them and paying a bit more attention as they come up again will raise your awareness the next time.

Think back to a time in your life when you were in control and understood everything that was going on. Life seemed to be motoring along smoothly. Somehow, your emotions and your energy levels were high, and you were able to achieve and get a sense of fulfilment.

I know that following my weight loss during my forties, and when I was in a very good exercise and eating routine, my emotions and energy were also at a high level. I was engaged, more motivated and just seemed to achieve more with my personal and my career life.

That has extended into my current day-to-day situation. I've successfully re-partnered and I'm extremely happy where I am now. My weight is maintained, I consider myself in a good, healthy routine and I'm very thankful for being able to reflect on the years where I did have difficulties, to enable me to make the changes necessary in all aspects of my life now.

There is no doubt that once you find your happy place or add to your happiness toolbox, you will feel a sense of self-control, and other people around you will recognise this.

You'll find that your thinking will become more focussed. One of the other benefits, once you have everything organised and have the capacity to cope with changes, is that your sleeping patterns will improve. Often clients of mine have been able to have dreams again, something that has been long forgotten.

The parasympathetic nervous system plays an important part while you're asleep, ensuring that you are restored and enable to move forward into the next day. Sleeping is one of the key elements to gauging how healthy you are. We all recognise that if you're able to fall asleep quite easily and have a restful sleep during the night, the next day will be so much easier.

Some of these strategies may not work for you, but my suggestion is you keep on trying them until you find out what works for you and do it repeatedly. Ten to fifteen minutes a day is all that is required. It's going to seem foreign initially, the first time that you do a mindfulness exercise, but it's just like trying anything new for the first time. My advice is to keep on trying. It's going to feel a little bit unnatural at first, but in time it will become easier.

3. Unlock Your Happiness Toolbox

Healthy options to take:

1. Pinpoint the stresses of your day-to-day or week-to-week calendar that you know that are distressing you and tackle them head-on. Break the larger issue down into bite size pieces. If it is a clutter or an organization issue, continue to chapter four.
2. Think back on a time in your life when you were in a good place, when you did have a sense of control and balance. Try to think about what it looked like for you, and how it felt. Write it down.
3. Select a mindfulness activity that suits your style and your personality that you know you can repeat, so that you can find that balance to enable your body to grow and restore.

Happiness is not something that comes readymade, it comes from your own actions.
Dalai Lama

4. Bust Your Midlife Clutter

Out of clutter, find simplicity. From discord, find harmony. In the middle of difficulty, find opportunity.
Albert Einstein

THERE'S SOMETHING ABOUT making your bed each day that sets you up for the next 24 hours. It's the fact that you've started and finished something that you've set out to achieve each day. While making your bed may not be a popular task for some, it's the act of starting and finishing something that gives most people a sense of satisfaction.

How many times have you set out to do something, and distractions have got in your way, or the environment around you has been so confusing that you haven't been able to achieve that task?

During this chapter, we'll look at ways for you to gain control of your everyday life, for you to avoid the stress of searching for things, which will ultimately save you time. You can become more reliable to yourself and to others around you, and you may even save some money!

I can hear some of your excuses: you don't have time to organise yourself. However, it has been proven that if you're more organised, in the long-term you can actually be more efficient.

> *For every minute spent in organising, an hour is earned.*
> **Benjamin Franklin**

Something happens in the brain once you organise a part of your life. There is a sense of relief that comes from doing that small bit of organising that gives you clarity for the period afterwards. One of the main causes of anxiety is being disorganised, and we all know how overwhelming it is when you just can't find something. For others, 'organised chaos' is the norm. When someone moves something unbeknown to you it causes friction.

Being organised, by comparison, gives you a sense of being more in control of your life.

For most, being organised reduces overall stress. In the last chapter, we covered stress, and its impact on your physiology. In order for us to be in balance, being organised can be one of the key factors to maintaining a healthy mind and subsequently, body.

Being organised and getting rid of the clutter will also give you time to enjoy the valuable things in life. Again, it's the enjoyable things in life that give you the restoration and growth that you need for your body to restore.

Once you bust your clutter, you become more reliable. It gives you a sense of 'no fuss freedom' that things will run smoothly for you. The number of times that you need to stop, look, and search will be greatly decreased.

One of the things that I've heard from other people over my career is that I'm an extremely organised person. Some days I don't feel like it, but I think looking over my career and my family life, I have been extremely organised, and I'm grateful to my both of my parents for this. My parents had a military background; my mother was also a private secretary after she left the army. The importance of being organised was ingrained in me.

Having said that, I did grow up in quite a carefree, loving family environment. My parents laid the foundations of work and play. It gave me a strong understanding of the sweet and sour in life; to achieve balance you need to go through challenges in order to enjoy the good times.

Later on, as I moved forward in my nursing career, being organised and balancing family life, home life, and at times incorporating study, was sometimes challenging. Making priorities and choosing what to put aside and include were a big part of getting organised.

Where do you start?
Where do you start with all of this?

In my view, there are four keys to succeeding in being organised.

1. Break it down

Identify what area or situation you want to declutter. What is most concerning you about the clutter that you live in each day? What aspect of it is challenging you the most? Even though you may feel a bit overwhelmed by the size of it, the key is to break it down into small pieces.

Let's take the example of a household that has too much physical clutter around the home environment. Breaking this down and doing one room in one month may be a realistic goal for you, or perhaps tackling one room each week for however many rooms that you have in the house. Say you have eight rooms: you're going to have a clutter-free environment this time next year. By breaking down whatever the most impacting clutter is for you into smaller chunks, you can manage it a whole lot better. You can be in a better place to visualise how that's going to look in the long term.

2. Use 'project thinking'

One way that I encourage my clients, is rather than organising your calendar into time, to break it up into 'project thinking' rather than time management. In that bigger project, you can break things down into smaller actions. I'll give you an example. Using the above example, to apply project thinking to your house decluttering, your project would be, 'declutter my house'. You could then list actions under each room. Each room might have its own set of actions: an action could be to clean out one of the cupboards or one of the drawers or a bookshelf each day. They would be the actions that you want to complete each day in order for you to complete that room as a stepping stone to the project completion of decluttering your house.

A similar theme is to organise things in your house so that you gather 'like' pieces of equipment or put together in a box or a container of things used for a task, so that you can grab the container and you know everything connected with that activity is in the box. For example, everything to fix your bike, including spare tubes, batteries, and the pump, could be stored in one hard plastic, weatherproof box which could then be kept neatly in the garage, rather than pieces spread all over the place.

You haven't put any times to these, they're just actions, and as you complete the actions, you can tick them off as you go. When you accomplish the decluttering of one room, you can reward yourself, such as watch a movie or have a relaxing bath.

3. Use colours

Colour coding is extensively used in large organisations to organise systems. It enables everyone in these organisations to readily find pieces that they might need to complete a task. In healthcare, there is a universal colour code designating what type of waste is produced and outlining how it should be disposed of correctly.

The same principle can be used around the home, for each individual, or for grouping similar things together so everyone can find them easily.

4. The 1, 2, 4 method

The fourth strategy that I wanted to explain to you is very similar to the project and action list, but this is a daily activity where you're using the 1, 2, 4 method. I've used this strategy for a long time now and I've found it works well for prioritising your actions throughout your day.

Rather than just listing your actions on a to-do list, place a number 1 next to the most challenging thing that you want to accomplish in the day. You know that it's going to take greatest amount of your energy and most of your time for that day.

The '2' is for two other things that you want to do that day that you know are going to take less time and action, but a little bit of effort to get through. Timewise, they could take ten minutes to half an hour, but these are two things that you want to accomplish, and they are the second priority to get done during the day.

The '4' list comprises the smaller things that you can accomplish that day – things that are going to take five or ten minutes to do, and if you don't get them done today then it's not of great importance. They are things that could be postponed to tomorrow, but you can challenge yourself to try and get through your entire 1, 2, 4 list for the day.

Diaries and journaling

How many of you, at the end of a year or financial year, really look forward to going out and buying a brand-new diary? This is the diary that's going to get you more organised. What I've found over the years is I've always gone back to a very similar looking diary for myself.

The look and the feel of it, the way it's organised, for me I think it's the familiarity that makes it easier to use. A lot of people now use diaries on the phone or their electronic devices and they link all sort of things.

What I've found though is that if your phone dies, or your computer breaks, then that information is lost, and it then becomes burdensome to remember passwords for retrieval. There is something about the written word that gives you that sense of control, and for me, a sense of accomplishment.

4. Bust Your Midlife Clutter

Be realistic

You've only got roughly 14 hours a day to do things, so being realistic in your priority management is important in ensuring that you don't enter a state of being overwhelmed and stressed. Being realistic is being kind to yourself.

The important thing here is to take ownership of where you want to take back control over your life, and once you've worked through a few strategies and tried them a number of times, you will develop a sense of control and reduce the stress that you've been feeling.

Some of this organisation transfers into your lifestyle, and over time these will become habits – great habits to have moving forward. The good thing about this is if you've got children or grandchildren around you, they will see that you're a very organised person. They will aspire to be like you, and you will create another generation of organised individuals.

Healthy options to take:

1. Discover what is most distressing to you about your environment and start there.
2. Think about your projects as organizing your energy, rather than thinking about time management.
3. Look at the value of colour coding to separate things or use bags and boxes to put similar things together.
4. Use the 1, 2, 4 method of prioritizing your activities each day.
5. Use a diary and/or journal to document your activities. There is something about the written word that just gets it done.

Organised people are just too lazy to look for things.
Unknown

5. Diet Is A Dirty Word

Science has not identified the healthiest way to eat. In fact, it has come as close as possible (because you can't prove a negative) to confirming that there is no such thing as the healthiest diet. To the contrary, science has established quite definitively that humans are able to thrive equally well on a variety of diets. Adaptability is the hallmark of man as an eater. For us, many diets are good while none is perfect.
M. Fitzgerald (2014) Diet Cults

THE WORLD OFFERS a plethora of reasons why you should choose one diet over another. It appears every season. Every year, there is a new diet trend linked with the latest science, and people fall for it. Promoted by the hottest actor of the time with the newest scientific breakthrough or the link to whatever health condition, product or superfood that is being promoted.

Let's break down the facts behind the most common approaches to eating so that you can make an informed decision. Your diet should follow you, it should suit you and your circumstances, and should inform your decisions to get your mojo back.

I'm going to help by giving you an understanding of a handful of diets that are in the headlines at the moment. I'm also going to mention a reliable resource to help work out your needs, so that you can be more informed about your nutrition. We're going to look at strengthening your relationship with food without depriving you.

When I looked at my diet in my forties I was really confused. There were mixed messages out there, and I was overwhelmed by the amount of information that was available. I did give in to a shake and supplement company for a period of time, but what it did not teach me thoroughly was the value of looking at all the other aspects of food preparation besides its nutritional value. The social aspect of shopping, storing, and the art of preparing a meal. The forward planning and discussion about meals with those that you live with, as an opportunity to share and swap ideas.

I feel embarrassed now to admit that I came to the late realisation that we have a gastrointestinal tract for a purpose: to break down, digest and absorb the nutrients in our foods. We grind our food in order for the stomach acids work on the contents, we ferment and absorb in our gut naturally. Any wonder that the nutrition and weight loss industry is worth multi million dollars to the worldwide market. The Australian weight loss industry is worth $643 million each year.[3] We are vulnerable.

---

3. Allday, A, 2013, 'Steadily expanding: health consciousness and growing obesity drive industry growth', *IBISWorld Industry Report S9512 Weight loss services in Australia*, viewed September 2018, <http://collegeofweightmanagement.com.au/wp-content/uploads/2015/06/S9512-Weight-Loss-Services-in-Australia-industry-report.pdf>.

5. Diet Is A Dirty Word

The fact is it's only going to get bigger with the obesity epidemic likely to be the number one health issue in the future. We're now seeing the obesity epidemic taking over our children and there's a lot of work being done on developing role model mothers, because the mothers play the most instrumental part in a child's upbringing. That could undoubtedly be argued, but overall it is the mother in the home that makes a lot of the decisions about food, nutrition and lifestyle, and act as role models for the younger children in the family.

We now know quite categorically the link between poor nutrition and the development of pre-disease states leading to Type 2 diabetes, heart disease and the organ failure. There is also new research coming out looking at the link between behaviour disorders and mental illnesses.

One of the risks of having or participating in what we call a 'fad diet' is that even though they may be based on what appears to be well-founded science, a lot of them (in my view) lack certain nutritional elements that are essential for overall wellbeing for the long term.

And you're not alone with the confusion. It's one of the reasons why people don't stay on a nutrition plan. They are overwhelmed with choices and dubious facts about different diets, and a lot of them are restrictive and unsustainable.

Whichever path you choose to take with your nutrition plan, you want to pick something that is suitable for all situations and scenarios, from cooking at home, to eating out, to making sensible choices in restaurants and cafe situations. Pick a diet that is flexible enough to move with your lifestyle. You don't want to 'fall off the wagon' because you have decided to enjoy yourself!

What I've found is that if you keep it as simple as possible, you're likely to have more success. Another thing that I've found is that if you make simple changes to your diet, and sustain them, it will make a big difference over the long term.

I often hear people say they are committed to a diet, that they've put so much time, energy and money into the diet, that they don't want to give it away. My response to that is, what is your long-term goal? Is the path you've chosen sustainable over a long period of time? And does it actually suit your family and social circumstances? The choices that you make need to fit in with your family lifestyle and budget, because even though you are looking after yourself, you do need to make those considerations for everyone.

Some words, like 'diet', 'eating plan', 'formula', and 'blueprint for nutrition', can catch your eye, but really it comes down to a lifestyle nutrition plan for you, your family and your social circumstances.

Fad diets

Fad diets are everywhere, so be wary of any diets that are endorsed by a celebrity. Become educated and informed about the diets and think about your overall nutrition plan. Think about the reason behind why the celebrity is appearing in the advertisements. It's probably not in your best interests, but in the celebrity's – it's more about the publicity, the dollar incentives and endorsements.

The Paleo Diet

This diet is likened to eating like a caveman thousands of years ago, prior to the rise of agriculture. It involves avoiding anything remotely modern, including grains, processed foods, dairies, pulses, salt and sugar.

The theory of this is that you eat more protein and healthy fats, and that this will sort everything out. It is based on the theory that our genes have not evolved over time and you need to keep in mind how long our ancestors from hundreds of years ago lived.

My view on this is that even between generations we do have adaptation. You look at generations over the time and you can see the genetics between a line of families, but they're all different.

The same difference happens in our gastrointestinal system, it does have the ability to adapt. This is where we have so many people now 'dependent' on processed foods such as sugar, which brings me to ...

The Sugar Free Diet
The reasoning behind this diet is that we don't need the simple sugars that are now conveniently available to us. The idea is that the added fructose sugars, such as corn syrup, are bad for us, and that the unused sugars that we ingest in these types of foods get stored ultimately as fat. Cutting back is highly recommended. Keeping complex carbs in our diets is essential for the different energy systems that we use. Did you know that the brain's only energy source is glucose?

When I cut out processed sugars from my diet, I know that not only do I feel better, but my skin is much better, and I seem to have more overall sustainable energy throughout the day.

The Low Carb Diets, Keto or the Atkins Diet
These diets are based on using a lower proportion of carbohydrates and a higher proportion of healthy fats. It mainly consists of lean meat, fish, eggs, any vegetables that are grown above the ground and natural fats like butter.

This diet also avoids any sugary and starchy foods, such as breads, pasta, rice, beans and potatoes. The theory behind this is that your blood sugar levels drop and subsequently less insulin is released; this results in the body sourcing stored fat for energy.

The Atkins diet is generally done in four stages, which produces a state of *ketosis,* and then reintroducing the good carbohydrates, ultimately working your way through to be on a maintenance diet.

Intermittent Fasting
There is some thought, also based on the caveman days, which suggests that going for a long period of time without any food kick-starts the metabolism into breaking down food products better when we eventually consume them.

My view is that sustainable energy throughout the day can be achieved by eating sensibly and by having a good night's sleep. A good night's sleep resets, (as I've mentioned in chapter three) rests the body and restores us so that we can produce healthy cells to regenerate and revitalise.

This occurs naturally if you have your meals spaced throughout the day, with waking and sleeping taking place at the same or similar time every day, so that you have between 11 and 12 hours of fasting while you're asleep at night. This, in my opinion, is natural intermittent fasting that fits with the natural day cycle.

The 5–2 Diet or the 2–5 Diet (depending on which resource you use)
This diet is where you slash your calorie intake for two days a week. The diet claims to not only produce weight loss but decrease blood pressure and cholesterol. Some improvement in memory and cognitive function has been

found, and studies done in obese women may be slightly biased towards getting a result. This is very similar to the intermittent fasting diet.

How to spot a fad diet ten kilometres away:
- It usually has strict rules about what you can and can't eat.
- It usually excludes a food group, such as carbohydrates.
- It generally implies that by changing your food intake, or a particular food group intake, that it can change your body chemistry.
- It often promises a quick-fix solution to your weight loss.
- It can suggest that there are magic food combinations that make this diet work.

Fad diets and health problems
Because of the restrictive nature of some of these fad diets, health problems may evolve. Before you start on an eating plan, it's always recommended that you consult your general practice doctor, and of course, some specific conditions do require a nutritionist's input for specific dietary modifications. Some of the signs that you may be compromised if you are on a fad diet include symptoms such as dehydration, weakness and fatigue, constipation or diarrhoea, headaches, nausea and vomiting, and anything unusual that is not 'you'.

If you're on one of these fad diets, one question I would ask is, if these diets are so effective for weight loss, then why are there so many new ones popping up? Surely, if one diet worked then it would be around and supported for a long time? While you might be looking for a fast way to lose weight, there will always be no shortage of fad diets that are available in the market, because their creators know that you are vulnerable. They might provide short-term results, but as I said before, the long-term (twenty-plus years) results are generally not included.

They deprive you of essential nutrients and the only real solution is a balanced eating program that encompasses other areas of your lifestyle.

In my view, everything in moderation is the best plan.

So, what happens when we age?

In general, as we age, our metabolism slows down. Our muscle mass decreases and our ability to burn calories becomes less efficient, we just can't eat like we're twenty-five years old anymore. We generally develop a decreased appetite as our basal metabolic rate naturally declines.

What to do to stay healthy:
1. Don't add salt.
2. Drink more water (unless it's otherwise contraindicated).
3. Limit alcohol.
4. Decrease or eliminate saturated fats.
5. Increase healthy fats.
6. Consume micronutrient-dense foods (vitamins and minerals: eat your greens).
7. Increase calcium and vitamin D.
8. Increase proteins, animal and plant-based proteins.
9. Watch your portions.
10. Decrease your simple sugars.
11. Eat complex carbohydrates in the first half of the day.

12. Freeze leftovers for lunch the following day.
13. Eat fresh where possible, then frozen, then canned, then dried.
14. Eat raw where possible, followed by steamed, baked, boiled and lastly pickled.
15. Avoid processed foods.
16. For a quick meal, buy healthy, frozen meal and add frozen green beans or peas for bulk.
17. Prepare food in bulk and freeze in small portions.
18. When dining out, ask for gravy and sauces on the side.
19. If chips are included in a purchased meal, ask them to be replaced with vegetables.
20. Eat an apple or a pear while you are shopping.
21. Bonus: Enjoy low fat Greek yoghurt with fresh fruit for a regular dessert option.

My top nine tips to blend a healthy eating habit into your life:

1. Remove all unwanted foods and drinks from your kitchen.
2. Eat at home prior to doing the grocery shopping.
3. Make sure you keep hydrated, always carry a water bottle.
4. Shop mainly from the outer rim of the supermarket.
5. If you know you're going to be busy the following day, make enough dinner for your lunch the following day.
6. Purchase a great lunch bag that will keep your lunches cool and transportable.
7. A weekly food prep session will save you time.
8. Switch to a small plate for serving size.
9. Conserve your treats to larger celebration times.

Reliable information

A reliable source that I've used over the years is the CSIRO's resources for nutrition. There are many books readily available based on scientific evidence.

The recipes include all five food groups, with a huge emphasis on eating vegetables and healthy dressings involving vinegars with citrus, nuts, herbs and spices.

Using these recipes, I have gained a better knowledge of food and an enhanced enjoyment of cooking. I never enjoyed cooking as a child, and through my adult life and family responsibilities, I saw it more as a chore. My relationship with food has changed over the last few years.

I've re-educated myself in cooking and combining all these foods and I've developed a form of mindfulness, losing myself in the kitchen. I use it as a way of unwinding and relaxing, while keeping my brain active by cooking enjoyable nutritious meals for myself and my family.

Let's talk about energy

We all know that we get the energy from our foods. Each of the macronutrients in our foods provides a specific amount of energy; this is metabolised by our body and used to give us movement and give the body baseline energy for the activities that we need to do every day.

It's a little bit more complex than 'energy in' versus 'energy out' gives you the 'plus or minus' for your weight, but in general, a good, well balanced diet with moderate exercise can lead to some weight loss, weight maintenance and leaner muscle mass.

5. Diet Is A Dirty Word

How much energy is contained in the macronutrients in our foods?

Fat is the most concentrated energy source. It contains nine calories per gram. Protein contains four calories per gram, so too do carbohydrates and alcohol (I have included that as a food group because it's interesting), which contain seven calories per gram.

Remember, we are talking energy alone, rather than the properties of the food substances and how they are metabolised.

Carbohydrates

It's well known that carbohydrates provide the body with the calories that it needs or the fuel that we need for our energy expenditure. The foods that contain the most carbohydrates include fresh fruit and vegetables, legumes and grains, breads, cereals, rice, pasta and noodles, and low-fat milk and yogurts.

These foods are also rich in vitamins and minerals and are low in fat. They should be included as part of your healthy eating plan.

The simple sugars contained in soft drinks and sweets are another source of carbohydrates, but these contribute a higher calorie load without the essential vitamins and minerals.

Protein

Protein is a larger, more complex and essential nutrient for every cell in your body. The body needs it to make, maintain and restore its new tissues and cells, and proteins can be classified as being found in either animal or vegetable products.

Animal Proteins
These include meat, chicken, dairy products, eggs and fish.

Vegetable Proteins
These include seeds, lentils, soy milk, peas, tofu and nuts.

Proteins are essential to maintaining lean muscle mass, particularly in our midlife years, to ensure that we have strong, lean muscles to protect our joints and to provide the mobility that we need.

Fats

Without a doubt, we need fats to maintain some of our normal body processes. Fats protect our organs; they help us absorb nutrients and some vitamins and they also help us in some hormonal production.

The healthier versions are the unsaturated fats that are found in things such as olive oils, nuts, seeds, and avocado. Saturated fats found in sausages, biscuits, cream, cakes and fried food are not good for our systems.

Healthy options to take:

1. Make grocery shopping, food preparation and the whole relationship with food a part of your lifestyle. Incorporate it into your very being and understand and appreciate the work that goes into producing fresh fruit and vegetables. Enjoy the love and passion of food and the feel, texture and aromas of cooking. Learning how to cook again has certainly been a big part of my whole approach to healthier eating.
2. Being organised is important; give yourself the opportunity to spend the time in the kitchen, try to make it a relaxing past-time.
3. There's more to eating than just a nutrition plan in my view; it's a whole lifestyle choice involving making better decisions for the most important person in your life, which is you.

6. Your Movement Mojo

The only workout you'll regret is the one that didn't happen.
Bob Harper

WHAT WORKED FOR YOU in your thirties and forties will not give you the same results into your fifties. Your body has changed and will continue to change. Let's look at what's happening and choose realistic movement options for your longer-term health.

In this chapter we'll deal with body changes and how you can incorporate some exercise modifications to incorporate those body changes.

We know that a sedentary lifestyle, restricted movement or being immobile can lead to longer term health problems.

We know that older adults who remain physically active are stronger into their sixties and seventies, and we also know that they recover at a faster rate from illnesses or physical injury if they continue to remain active.

Your reasons for staying active may be vastly different to what your reasons were in your thirties and forties, and if you've never exercised before, now is the time for you to incorporate some healthy movement or activity in your life to prevent the longer-term problems that we see in epidemic proportions all around the world, placing strain on our healthcare system.

Strain on our healthcare system not only impacts our economy, it impacts on everyone in their day to day functions, because ultimately, we all must pay taxes to contribute towards the long-term expense of looking after chronic health conditions in our healthcare systems.

Not only that, it's vital that we act as role models for younger people and that we leverage the younger generations – full of vitality and energy – by drawing on their enthusiasm to motivate ourselves to be active if we previously have not been.

For some, exercising may not have been an enjoyable part of your life, but there are ways of incrementally introducing it into your lifestyle as part of your plan. Some of you are probably saying that you're quite happy with the way that you are, and you don't feel the need to improve or increase any exercise. Remember in chapter two, we talked about the stress response and how staying in your comfort zone for a prolonged period leads to lethargy and fatigue? We need the stimulation of movement to get the blood flowing and to awaken our body systems.

But there are other benefits of exercising that are more than just physical. Exercise lifts your mood; it takes you to a place where you can forget about things for a while, it can increase your energy levels and just make you feel better.

I have a question for those who are happy in their comfort zone. If you don't incorporate some aspect of movement and activity into your life now, what is your life going to look like in ten years? That's a hard question that some people just really don't want to answer. They may already know the answer from looking at older siblings or parents and seeing how their lives have played out.

That thought process formed a part of my epiphany when I walked that flight of stairs and suddenly realised that I wasn't the fit person that I had thought I was. My body had got to a stage where my unhealthy choices at the time were catching up with me. I thought that it was OK to cheat a little because I was so active. I knew then I needed to make a decision. Yes, that was in my forties, but certainly now into my fifties if I do let things slide, I'm again reminded of how life could be if I don't continue along the healthier path.

Now, with a healthier mind-set and approach, my attitude towards exercise is that it's a part of my lifestyle that I incorporate into every day where I can.

Some of you might be already on an exercise program or a regime that you're quite happy with and that's fantastic. What I would suggest that you do with that program is ask yourself two key questions.

1. Is it sustainable for you in the longer term, over the next five to ten years? Think about the physical, economic and social impacts.

2. Are you still going to enjoy that type of activity over the next five to ten years?

If your answer to those two questions is 'yes', fantastic! You're on a great track, keep going.

If the answer to those questions is 'doubtful' or 'no', then I would suggest that you probably do some research into finding what sort of exercise you would enjoy to sustain you well into your fifties and sixties.

I'm using the word exercise quite freely, you can replace it with words such as mobility, movement, lifestyle, getting active, just getting out there and moving.

One of the key things as we get older is that we do have quite a lot of wisdom, which means that sometimes we don't take the advice that is readily available to us. Keeping an open mind, understanding where your body is now and listening for advice from exercise specialists that you trust would be valuable to move you forward.

As I said before, if you are on an exercise plan or have goals that are ticking those boxes for you, then that's fantastic, keep going. But the big focus is really on incorporating activity and movement into your lifestyle and making those choices for the key aspects of what we know deteriorates over the midlife years and beyond. It's not all doom and gloom. I hear a lot of clients being surprised at how much they now enjoy their new programs or lifestyle choices; they feel freer, more relaxed about their choices.

The number one thing is you need to enjoy what you're doing. Back in chapter one we looked at your reasons for maintaining your weight; your motivating drive. Your reasons for being on this journey are relevant to your exercise program.

What motivates you to get out the door could be the same thing – it could be the same thing you have in mind, that you're wanting to get out and enjoy life, to experience life. Once you enjoy every moment you can be the active parent, grandparent and son or daughter that you want to be.

The physiological changes that occur as we age

We know that we lose lean muscle mass and we also decrease our bone density as we age. In chapter five we looked at key nutritional tips for incorporating into our nutritional plans to ensure that we have enough nutrients on board to cope with our changing bodies. The same applies to exercise, and the movement that we should be encouraged to practice as either part of a structured program or as a lifestyle choice.

Other things that deteriorate over time are the ability to perform coordinated and balanced movements, and the capacity or thought processes for thinking through or forward planning our movements, for example with daily requirements such as negotiating stairs, picking up something from the floor, or navigating our way through a crowd.

Our senses

Think about the physiological changes that happen with our eyesight, hearing and perception, which cause our sense of balance to be compromised. We may not be as sharp as we were in our earlier years. Some of you in your fifties may be thinking, 'No, this is not happening to me.' You may be in complete denial that this is happening. But it does happen, it will happen and the reality of this is that you do need to incorporate some of these aspects into adjusting what you are doing.

Regular eye and hearing function tests are widely accessible. Of course, if you are having balance issues, it pays to get an assessment from your general practitioner.

Bones and connective tissues

In my forties, when I took up half-marathon running, I had no idea at the time that I would be continuing to run into my fifties. It unfortunately stopped short in the last four years due to a chronic Achilles condition, so much so that I've had to adjust what I'm doing to maintain my activity into my fifties. Currently, my approach is to make decisions for the long-term regarding my lifestyle and movement choices. For my long-term benefit, I aim to remain active so that I can continue to move and prevent injury well into my later years.

What I have learned since is the concept of 'training age'. I have never been a long-distance jogger. When I embarked on my goal to run a half marathon, I mistakenly assumed that running a half marathon would be the same as running four lots of five-kilometre runs in a row. I escalated my weekly longest run too rapidly for my body at the time, over a 12-month period. Some of the increments were quite dramatic, and looking back on it, I pushed myself 'beyond the pain', as you are often encouraged to do in running circles.

My advice now is to listen to your body and adjust what you are doing.

I'm not saying don't choose jogging or running as an option, in fact they are excellent methods of incorporating cardiovascular exercise. But what I do recommend is that you start slowly and build slowly to your desired distances. Follow a beginner program, readily available on the internet, and be aware of your body changes along the way.

As we age, our joints begin to stiffen, and it is vital to keep them moving. If you do have osteoarthritis or a joint issue that impacts on your ability to do any type of walking, jogging or cycling, then water activities may be a better option for you. There are several different types of classes or squads that you can join specifically designed for older adults.

One of the key things that I've allowed myself to do is to be kind to myself and give myself permission to say, 'Hey, running longer distances is not for me', and the high intensity exercise that I used to do in my thirties and forties is not the path that I could picture myself continuing with. Low and moderate intensity options, such as walking, jogging two to five kilometres, cycling, swimming, dancing and resistance training seem to be more attractive, and I've certainly incorporated them into my life with success.

Be a midlife social butterfly

Isn't it great to get with a group of friends to be able to combine some activity with socialising? It not only improves our happy zone, but feeds and motivates others as well as yourself in maintaining a good routine regarding exercise.

There's a lot of evidence to say that people who exercise in groups as they get older maintain that path and enjoy it more. The social interaction becomes important for support in our older years.

Financial considerations

Finances can play a part in being active. But whether your budget allows for a high-end solution or whether it doesn't allow for any monetary or limited funds for keeping active, it doesn't matter.

It's all about where you want to be and how you want to remain active.

Quite often I see clients that spend a lot of money enlisting in a program, or join an expensive gym, and they begrudgingly attend sessions and classes. They often walk out just feeling totally depleted and embarrassed.

Alternatively, some people do need money motivation to keep them going. They've invested a sum of money, so they want to get their money's worth and do quite well. So, it really comes back to: what are your key motivators?

What type of exercise would suit you?

Firstly, pick an exercise or an activity that you really enjoy doing and make that the focus of your movement plan.

As we get older we know that high intensity exercise can be done, but really you should be leaning towards a lower impact type of activity so that you're preserving the strength of your joints.

Having said that, it is quite controversial. If you have developed strong, supportive, connective tissue around your ankles and knees, you may be able to continue to do those types of exercises. Again, it comes back to 'training age'.

Incorporating a low to moderate impact option may be a better choice, using low impact exercises as part of a cardio, strength or resistance program to preserve the longevity of your knees, ankles and hips.

Such exercises include brisk walking, cycling and swimming. Dancing is a good option as well, as it evokes a love or passion for music as well as movement and the sensation of feeling free. It provides a low impact cardio when done for a period. Besides, it can be a lot of fun.

Exercise frequency

We read and hear that thirty minutes a day is all that is needed. More important is the quality of the movement that you are doing, and for what purpose. Thirty minutes strolling around the block will be great for your emotional wellbeing, but it won't move body fat or create the lean protective muscles essential in these years.

Seek out a plan, or (shock, horror!) ask for help from a trainer who understands the aging body and your unique situation. As I have said, incorporate what you love about movement into your plan.

For example, a weekly long walking hike might be in your plan, but for you to achieve this for relaxation, there would need to be some sessions during the week building up your leg muscles to train or sustain you for this. Interval stair walking and dancing that involves some squat and lunge moves could be an option.

What about stretches?

Stretching and mindfulness activities such as yoga, Pilates, and tai chi are excellent choices as well. They are known to yield great results in creating calm and will strengthen the body, improve circulation and breathing, and play a great role in curbing mental health conditions.

One disappointing thing that I have experienced as a trainer is that people do not value stretching enough. When we are young and supple, its generally thought that this is a waste of time. However, as we age, we can feel how beneficial these types of activities are, and the results they give in soothing our bodies. Take ten or fifteen minutes to stretch after each activity and enjoy the benefits.

Anyone who has trained with my partner Nigel and I, knows how seriously we take stretching, and our sessions are not complete until this is done thoroughly. Besides, it just feels good!

Healthy options to take:

1. For those of you already jogging or running, switch to interval training at least twice a week and focus on your form. Like any exercise that you do, if you have great form, the risk of injury will be minimised for the short and long term. For those that are not, incorporate walking, cycling or swimming into your week. The interval and strength training can be combined with cycling or swimming as well.

2. Complement this with a compound bodyweight strength session. There's no need for a gym; you can use your own bodyweight. Incorporate two to three focused stretch sessions and you're sure to be on a winner. Modified exercises can be learned for incorporating all your muscle groups.

3. Remember the 10% guide: by increasing any elements such as intensity or time by no more than 10% each week and over a long period of time with consistency and patience, you will succeed.

4. The key tip is to enjoy what you do. If you're not enjoying what you're doing, try something else. Think about a group sport or an active hobby instead. It's best to do it with friends.

5. Stay consistent. Keeping consistent over time will bring you results. I liken staying with an exercise program to cutting your hair: You've made the decision to make a change, but the only way you're going to keep that hairstyle is to go back and maintain it.

Yoga is a metaphor for life. You have to take it really slowly. You can't rush. You can't skip to the next position. You find yourself in very humiliating situations, but you can't judge yourself. You just have to breathe and let go. It is a workout for your mind, your body and your soul.
Madonna

7. Aging with Dignity

Being a healthy woman isn't about getting on a scale or measuring your waistline... we need to start focussing on what matters – on how we feel, and on how we feel about ourselves.
Michelle Obama

EXPRESSING YOURSELF AS UNIQUE is a wonderful thing to do, especially as you mature. I fondly think back to my grandparents and great aunts and uncles and remember aspects of their characters and mannerisms that I admired. It's this of kind memory that I want to leave with my grandchildren and I'm sure I'm not alone.

In this chapter, I want to help you limit any doubts you have, to get rid of those limiting beliefs that impact on your ability to put yourself forward as the best person you can be.

We look around the community these days and we can pull out from a crowd someone who walks with confidence amidst the grey hairs. I have aspired to live up to the likes of my own idols, some of whom are people that are in the public eye, such as Helen Mirren, and strong Australian women such as Olivia Newton-John, and Sarah Jane Henderson, the fabulous Australian outback property owner and author.

They stand out in my mind as being strong, empowered women who are full of confidence and with a good self-image, all while staying true to themselves.

Why is it important to age with dignity and poise? In my view, the answer is to gain respect from themselves first, then others. I believe that someone who walks into a room and can carry themselves with their head held high and their shoulders back, speaking confidently and with wisdom, gains respect very quickly from the crowd that they're in. It's an attractive quality to have.

Take time to identify or think about those that you admire. Have a think about their characteristics and their mannerisms. What attracts you to those people? What do you see about their personality or the way that they look and dress, the way that they carry themselves, the way that they speak, their views and how they articulate their views on life, that instantly attracts you to them?

For me, it's attributes such as calmness, being organised, having wisdom, knowledge and experience, having an air of confidence about them. Women who are quite decisive about themselves, while remaining gentle and calm. To a degree, they are assertive, but without the power or the ego behind that assertiveness. There's a sense of knowing the direction that they're heading.

7. Aging with Dignity

I often think about why I'm attracted to those types of people and I'd have to say that it's the influence that my parents had on me earlier in my life. They had such strong values about life and a view on treating people with respect and treating people equally. They were always respectful towards other people. My dad always carried himself with his head held high, he had a strong stature and a presence about him and when we were in a room full of people, others would come up to him and treat him with respect, which gave me the impression that he was thought of in a very positive light.

But I know that that stature didn't come automatically to Dad. He had to work very hard throughout his career to gain that presence and reputation amongst people.

One of the common traps that I see and advocate quite strongly against is when people heading towards their midlife years try to act and appear as though they're twenty years younger. The commercialism around staying young and looking young forever is a multi-million-dollar business. No wonder marketing is centred on trying to capture the essence of youth, trying to keep people looking and presenting as younger versions of themselves.

In my view, people can see through that. People can see how old you are, behind the dyed hair and the makeup and the cosmetic surgery that has taken place. They can see right through, and to me, someone who is more mature and presents themselves with wisdom and experience holds more value in my eyes.

> *It's ridiculous to pretend that we can stay young forever.*
> **Helen Mirren**

One way that I've consistently maintained my own sense of self is to reflect often. I'm a journal writer, but documenting and reflecting can occur in different ways: it can be achieved by looking at pictures, looking at videos, reflecting on your social media activity, and really probing the space for what your thoughts and feelings were around those memories, whether they are recent or older recollections.

Ask yourself questions repeatedly, what were you thinking and feeling at that time? Did you have a sense of control over what was happening? Explore your questions and your feelings around those pictures and journal entries.

Out of all those discussions with yourself, pull out some positive affirmations. Keep giving yourself affirmations about how valued and experienced you are, that you are valuable to the world, that you have a lot to offer others through your experience. Revel in others' positive feedback. Quite often when someone pays you a compliment, it's not within our culture to accept the compliment. I don't know why people do this. When someone pays you a compliment and it is genuine, thank them, because they are adding value to your own self-esteem bank.

If you're recognised for an achievement or for accomplishing something, really dwell on that sense of pride. Sometimes we do tend to get a little bit overwhelmed and embarrassed, but if we can think about the hard work that we've put into doing something and someone acknowledges that hard work and effort, really absorb that accolade.

One way to boost your self-esteem is to think of the success that you've had in the past that you hold dear to your heart.

For me, coming through my forties and achieving my dramatic weight loss and the sporting goals that I set for myself – running five half-marathons – I was stronger and fitter and healthier. There was nothing better than feeling like that.

And reflecting further back into my childhood and youth, my best year was Year Ten. Looking back on that year, I was absorbed in sport, I was absorbed in school life and had a good circle of friends. We had so much fun that year. It was a busy year and it went by in a flash, but looking back, that year I had a very high level of self-confidence.

More recently, travelling to central Australia for four weeks, Nigel and I found ourselves in a space of knowing that this is what we wanted to do. This is where we wanted to be for most of our leisure time, and if we could possibly make that happen, we would make our long-term choices to make this a reality.

From positive memories like these, think of yourself as being the producer of your own personal positive movie. What does your movie look like? Who is playing in the starring role and who do you have as the supporting actresses and actors? How does it play out? Is there a lot of activity and enthusiasm? Or is it a calm movie? What sort of setting is it in? What's the theme that's running through the movie? What's the message of your movie that you're getting out there?

This movie that you're developing should or could explore your good experiences and be a platform for you to be the star of the show. Taking this movie into the future, using some imagery and imagination, you can set the scene for producing positive outcomes for experiences that are lying ahead for you.

It's well known that imagery is a positive thing that can be used in all walks of life. If you do have an experience coming up that you're quite fearful of, using imagery can propel you forward and give you internal confidence. If you run the sequence through your head or act it out in a room prior to the event, it's amazing how much confidence you can achieve. Visualisation is used widely, in sports, in theatre, as a rehearsal for public speaking, or any other fear-inducing event that might be coming.

It combats all the negatives, so in the roleplaying you can run through some of the negative things that might happen and what your contingency plans could be for those events.

The 'M' word

I once heard a GP give a good explanation of female hormones and the statistics about how women experience menopause. She described it as being in thirds. One third of women go through menopause with very minimal disruption to their lives from their symptoms.

One third of women have mild symptoms that they choose to use lifestyle choices to manage (and I fit that category). And the final third of women have symptoms of menopause that do disrupt their lives immensely and must revert to specialist help with relevant treatment.

We all know that during menopause our hormone balance does become a little bit skewed, in that oestrogen, progesterone and testosterone levels are altered. It's these imbalances that cause some disruption to your physiology and subsequently everything else in your life. It's also commonly known that if your mind-set and your lifestyle choices are improved, that there is an improvement on the impact of these hormonal imbalances.

7. Aging with Dignity

> *My hair seems to have left my scalp and migrated to my face. Merry Menopause!*
> **Anon**

Traditionally and culturally, women have played a maternal, nurturing role in our society. If we continue to do so and are not seen as equal, then we are putting ourselves in a situation where our self-image may be compromised.

We are natural nurturers. But that shouldn't stop us from turning that into an asset to move us forward and give us the confidence in our abilities.

My view is that communication is key, and throughout our life changes – not only at menopause, but at other times – communication with our loved ones is vital in engaging the support that can build our self-image. Expressing our views about how we feel is important for others to be able to understand what's going on.

> *My grandma told me, 'The good news is, after menopause, the hair on your legs becomes really thin and you don't have to shave them anymore. Which is great, because it means you have more time to work on your new moustache!'*
> **Anon**

Cherish your uniqueness and your personality. I can hear you say that sometimes you feel stuck in a bit of a bog and can't move forward. My message is that you can take small, incremental steps and communicate with others around you to help you move forward.

What if other people pull you down? Well that's where your resilience, confidence in yourself and thinking back on positive experiences can pull you out and through that bog.

Remember in chapter one, I suggested you identify the five best people around you? Well, lean on those five people, lean on your five heroes to pull you through those times.

Understanding yourself and your reactions is vitally important to move forward and gain control. Be yourself, value your uniqueness, share with the world the beauty that you have within and shine like a bright star.

Healthy options to take:

1. Discover your past truths. Revisit your positive experiences; document them. It could be in photos, in videos, reflection journals, or creating your movie. Any aspects of documentation where you can look back with pride and pull the confidence factor from that to propel you forward.

All we can do is learn from the past and make peace with it.
Nicole Kidman

2. Build your value toolbox. Build those photos, journals, affirmations, or voice record what you want to say. Using music as an association to positive things can really help put your mind-set into a positive tone.
3. Understand the hormonal shifts that are happening at this time and allow yourself to go with the waves. If needed, consult a specialist to receive the treatment to help you feel back in control.

Cherish forever what makes you unique.
Bette Midler

8. Thrive Despite Chronic Conditions

IT WOULD BE NICE to say that getting to the age of fifty without a chronic condition would be ideal for everybody, but the reality is that some of us might have a chronic illness already and may have had it for some time. It can be hard but thriving despite this is possible. Managing the illness is key and having the right positive mind-set is paramount.

I must say that compliance to recommendations by health professionals should be utmost in your mind if you do have a chronic illness. Continuing to work with health professionals and using their support should be integral to the plan that you're undertaking.

> *Intelligence is the ability to adapt to change.*
> Steven Hawking

This chapter will explore the early symptoms of some of the more common chronic illnesses, otherwise known as 'pre-disease', to maximise your ability to identify if you have any signs or symptoms. We'll talk about the mind-set change of not primarily focussing on the adverse effects that the illness can bring to you, but rather focussing on the good aspects of your life. We'll work towards strengthening your resilience through the condition so that you may have every opportunity to thrive.

For some people, some of these illnesses can be all-consuming. The whole family becomes affected and needed to support you at home. But nevertheless, following the management plans that your health professionals have outlined for you to look after your illness is essential for you to move forward. Finding the joy within illness can move you forward and enable you to enjoy life around it.

A lot of people who have a family tendency for specific illnesses are quite fearful that they may be a candidate for going down the same path as their family members, but knowledge is power. Understanding the disease process, the signs and symptoms to look out for, will lead to an earlier diagnosis and get you started with interventions such as a healthier lifestyle, so that you can move forward and manage the disease appropriately.

Some people want to change, but like everyone else, can lack the motivation to change. Undertaking or maintaining a lifestyle change on top of managing an illness can seem insurmountable. But go back to chapter one where we looked at your reasons 'why'. Why would you want to make yourself heathier? We know if people with chronic diseases have a healthier lifestyle, they seem to manage their conditions much better, and bypass or delay a lot of the longer-term complications.

Some of the more common conditions

> Chronic diseases are long lasting conditions with persistent effects. Their social and economic consequences can impact on peoples' quality of life. Chronic diseases are becoming increasingly common and are a priority for action in the health sector. AIHW commonly reports on 8 major groups: arthritis, asthma, back pain, cancer, cardiovascular disease, chronic obstructive pulmonary disease, diabetes and mental health conditions.
> **Australian Institute of Health and Welfare, 2016.**

Let's go over some of the chronic conditions that are classified as 'chronic' according to health professionals, not only here in Australia but worldwide. I am not going to bamboozle you with too much science, just give you a basic understanding. We know that some of these diseases are induced by poor lifestyle choices which lead to obesity, and subsequently the development of some of conditions.

The chronic illnesses that we're going to talk about include diabetes, cancer, renal insufficiency, and heart disease. Mental health is fast becoming one of the key aspects of modern day living, with more data being presented on the link between obesity, poor nutrition and mental health conditions. Let's go through each of the health conditions.

Diabetes
In Australia, one person every five minutes is diagnosed with diabetes, which equates to 280 people every day. This adds up to 1.7 million people in Australia having diagnosed diabetes. The number of people affected by diabetes, including those that are living with diabetes in their families, may be as high as 2.4 million people. Consider the carers

and loved ones within those families. The cost to Australian community is $14.6 billion. No wonder we're spending so much money investing in screening and preventing illnesses such as diabetes.[4]

There are two types of diabetes. Type 1 diabetes is usually diagnosed from a very early age and primarily involves children. Often referred to as juvenile onset diabetes, this is where the person is dependent on insulin to move glucose from circulation into the cells. The cause is usually due to damage to the pancreas and genetics seem to play a part. It is also believed that it may be an autoimmune type of disease, where the body's own system affects the pancreas. The treatment is primarily diet, exercise, and administering insulin to maintain the blood sugar levels within a normal range.

Type 2 diabetes, or adult onset diabetes, is where there is an inability of the cells to respond to insulin, so there's a decreased sensitivity to the insulin that is produced by the pancreas. The cause is predominantly poor diet and lifestyle factors, but genetics do play a part as well.

Poor nutrition and lifestyle factors leading to obesity is a large factor in the development of mature or adult onset type 2 diabetes. The treatment is based on nutrition and exercise modifications and possibly administering oral medication or hypoglycaemics. In some severe cases where there is uncontrolled type 2 diabetes, insulin may be needed to stabilise blood sugar levels.

In prediabetes you are generally found to be overweight and could be classified as obese. There could be some disorders of the lipid metabolism. There's an altered glucose metabolism,

---

[4]. Diabetes Australia, 2015. Viewed September 2018 <https://www.diabetesaustralia.com.au/diabetes-in-australia>

abnormal inflammatory processes and oxidative stress. There could be hypertension, and indeed that is one of the risk factors.

When you develop insulin resistance the resulting outcome is that there is increased sugar that is circulating in the system. If it is not used by the body it gets stored, resulting in increased adipose tissue and damage to vessels throughout the body. Longer term, this can result in complications such as ineffective wound healing, poor circulation, poor vision, renal and heart problems.

How does this affect the body and what should we be looking out for? Blurry vision, an increase in thirst or the frequent need to urinate. This the body's attempt to try to get rid of the excess sugars. Other symptoms include feeling tired or ill all the time, recurring skin or gum or bladder infections, dry and itchy skin, unexpected weight loss despite the oral intake or the diet that the person is consuming. Cuts or abrasions in the skin that are quite slow to heal, bruising and decreased sensation or loss of feeling in the feet, or tingling feet or toes add to the list of effects the disease can have.

Cancers
Cancer or malignancy can be generally defined into two categories. One is solid tumour malignancies and the other is the hemopoietic malignancies. Some of the solid tumours can be associated with poor lifestyle and dietary factors include throat cancer, cancer of the gastrointestinal system including the oesophagus, stomach, bowel, and cancers of the genitalia or urinary tract. There are also cancers of the bladder, the prostate in men, and the reproductive cancers in women, such as breast, uterine, ovarian or cervical cancer.

The hemopoietic malignancies are quite broad and they're specifically aligned with the type of blood cells that are involved. This is quite complex to explain, and blood borne cancers are usually related to other complex factors one of which could include lifestyle.

Cancer warning signs[5]

1. A sore that doesn't heal, changes colour or ulcerates or bleeds.
2. Any unusual bleeding or discharge from any opening in the body, e.g., blood in the urine, more heavy menstruation than usual or blood in the stools.
3. A lump or a swelling that has enlarged, which may or may not have pain associated with it.
4. Indigestion or difficulty in swallowing either fluids or foods, something may get stuck in the throat or a continual coughing after eating or drinking.
5. A change in the bowel or bladder habits, which generally persist for an extended period; we all know that a bladder infection can be quite painful, if it continues despite antibiotics it should be investigated.
6. Any changes in your skin, warts or moles and a good preventive measure is to go and get the free skin check once every six months.
7. A persistent cough or a voice that changes and stays changed or husky for more than two weeks; that should be investigated.
8. Unexplained fatigue or tiredness associated with an unexplained weight loss of 10% or more of your baseline weight, generally over a three to six-month time frame.

---

5. Adapted from Queensland Cancer Council, viewed September 2018 <https://cancerqld.org.au/cancer-prevention/early-detection/understand-your-body/>.

9. Persistent discomfort or pain in the abdomen, that there seems to be no logical answer for.
10. An unexplained fever, you've been tested for different infections and the fevers persist.

If any of these symptoms are present, seeing your general practitioner for further assessment/ongoing referral is essential.

Renal/Kidney Issues
Renal insufficiency is quite a broad term, but it can be a symptom of other conditions that could be underlying. Medical staff might want to investigate further if you should come to them with any of the early signs of renal insufficiency, for example unintentional weight loss, any nausea or vomiting that's not related to a potential food poisoning type of episode, generally feeling unwell, increased fatigue and headache, frequent hiccoughs and generalised itching (or its medical term, pruritis).

Heart Disease
Sometimes you can think of it as your 'heart in a slump'. One of the signs of this is hypertension; look out for persistent headaches either at the front or on the sides, any changes in visual disturbances, any nausea or vomiting, abdominal pain, low or no urine output that could be as a result of hypertension (which again relates to renal insufficiency), awareness of feeling stressed or anxious.

Bear in mind that sometimes people have no symptoms.

Normal blood pressure in an adult is the measurement of 120 on 80. Anything above that is considered to be hypertension. The different stages of hypertension should be investigated by your doctor.

Heart disease is increasing; it's interesting that people live longer with heart disease than they did thirty to forty years ago. There are risks factors as well as a hereditary component to the disease. Subcategories of heart disease include coronary heart disease and generalised heart failure. Underneath these come valve disease, any form of aneurysm, coronary artery disease, arrhythmias, right and/or left heart failure, cardiomyopathy and pericarditis.

Familial history is very important when you're looking at heart health. Know the early signs, such as changes in heart rate and rhythm, shortness of breath, palpitations, pain in the chest, either at rest or on exertion or exercise, and investigate as a matter of urgency.

Swelling in the hands and the feet may be a symptom as well. As you can see there are several signs and symptoms that fall across different types of chronic diseases.

There are many more chronic diseases, but too many to mention in this book. However, know the early signs and symptoms and what to look out for, and take yourself off to the GP to get yourself investigated. One of the key messages for this chapter is to live your life despite the chronic illness that you have, or if you think you might have a chronic health condition then get it checked out.

To live a fulfilling life, it is important to embrace who you are and move yourself forward, think about your positive attributes and stay informed about your disease process so that you can manage it appropriately.

Some of the key things that you can do is again build on your strengths and your values, referring to chapter two. A lot of people with chronic illnesses like to give back to the community somehow, showing gratitude to the community around them. This way some people get a sense of fulfilment and a sense of purpose for what they're doing with their lives.

In my situation, when Dad became unwell in my late teenage years, his attitude was that he was still alive, and he still had family around him that loved and supported him. Every day was a blessing that he loved and enjoyed. He loved having family time and his sense of purpose was his family. He kept himself busy and active mentally. He was very much into sport, and horse racing, so he kept his mind quite active on those two activities.

> **Healthy options to take:**
> 1. Become educated on the signs and symptoms of pre-disease.
> 2. Seek medical attention if you are concerned about any signs and symptoms.
> 3. If you do have or develop chronic illness, go back to your lifestyle choices and make some changes to enable you to thrive.

Follow the advice of your health professionals and embrace the other chapters in this book to live your best life.

Stephen Hawking is getting a divorce. That's scary. If the smartest guy in the world can't figure women out, we're screwed.
Jay Leno

9. Managing the Mother Juggle

MIDLIFE IS SEEN as the sandwich age where you're a parent, you're a grandparent, possibly a child of aging parents, you have senior roles at work or assume parental roles within your community groups and your social networks.

It just feels like everyone's turning to you for support and to provide guidance. Sometimes you just want to pull the plug and stop parenting.

The fact is that you **can** provide that support and guidance. You **can** manage what seems like keeping a number of balls in the air at the one time. The trick is to value your role within those community groups.

Value your input to your aging parents, value your input into your roles at work and within your own family, your community groups and that social network that you have. I am sure those community members value your input!

Let's explore in this chapter how you can be in control of your own life so that you can give value to those around you, and how valuing your own skills and attributes in those groups can bring profound self-confidence.

It's getting back to the idea of prioritising the important things in your life, making sure that you are achieving your goals and your ambitions while staying calm and neutral towards yourself. Be your authentic self so that you can put your best foot forward.

Value the inputs to those around you and understand your role in each of those scenarios without taking over the whole aspect of those groups. For example, we've all seen the busy mothers who want to take control of a group and do everything, only to be burnt out at the end.

Communication comes into play here, as well as understanding where you sit within that group and identifying other group members that you could delegate to.

Some of the parents that I speak to say they feel they have expectations on them, that it is their role and we falsely think that it is our role in society. Generations have been brought up to understand that parents are the ones to look up to, but it doesn't mean that you actually have to do everything for that group.

You need to question whether that is your expectation of yourself, or is it the expectation of the group? Again, key here is the communication within the group and identifying who does what within that group. Matching up the skills and identifying what each person enjoys doing can result in the group being viable and successful.

9. Managing the Mother Juggle

The benefit of getting this right is that you will find balance in your life. You'll value the time that you have, and you'll be able to spend it with those that you love. There will be an overwhelming sense of presence about you amongst your group that you will find satisfaction with.

You'll find peace in some of the tough decisions that you might need to make, and sometimes you do need to delegate things, knowing that they're not going to be done quite to the level that you want, but you can always go back and nurture and improve that delegated task.

Some people also say that they have no time for themselves, that they can't take time out and enjoy some of the things that they love. Again, balance comes into play. Sometimes just tweaking a few things can give you enough time to be able to go and do those things for yourself.

Some people feel like they're the knot in the bow tie, that they seem to have two or three different worlds that are circulating around them, and they feel like they're the knot in the middle holding the thing together.

Currently, there are so many blended families, it's the norm now that children attend schools where the parent community includes broken marriages and re-partnered families which need to work together.

> Since 1986, the proportion of couples cohabitating has more than doubled from 5.7 per cent to 12.4 percent in 2001.
> **Ministerial Taskforce on Child Support, May 2005**

What this means is that there are more children going between one household and the other. If managed correctly that works well, but when it's mismanaged there is commonly a difference of opinion. Quite often there is a juggle of conflict and responsibilities between the two biological parents and this can impact on the ability to manage those situations.

I know myself when I separated from my ex-husband that one week would feel full-on when I had the children with all the responsibilities, and the second week there would be this great big void.

I recall starting to walk and jog, and I utilised that downtime in that off week to recharge my batteries, to find myself again, to work through strategies where I was looking after myself a bit better.

At the other end of the scale, midlifers also contribute towards the health and welfare of their aging parents and extended families. These days we rarely have the families residing in the same residence.

Families are often disjointed, they can be interstate and in other countries around the world, so the logistics of looking after parents and being actively involved in their welfare when there's distance involved can cause quite a lot of distress and added stress in the nuclear family.

Those are just the care aspects: then there's all the other aspects that go with the other responsibilities. There's the financial situation, making decisions for loved ones or assisting loved ones in making decisions, working with them towards having a happy, elderly time of life and making sure that they're as comfortable as possible.

Extending this out to the community, sometimes when we do take on community responsibility, there is an expectation that the midlifer be the one that can take on the responsibility of holding a position on a committee or taking the lead in organising an event.

Somehow, it just defaults to that midlife group; it just seems that the busier you are, the more activities it is assumed you would be able to manage.

So, the trick for how to manage all of this is to have a sense of self-empowerment and to have the ability to say 'no'. Realise that in order for you to prioritise the important things in your life and value the input into your immediate nuclear family, you need to be able to not keep saying 'yes' to added responsibilities, and to walk away from that scenario knowing that you have made the right decision for your own wellbeing.

Most people do understand when you highlight that you have other family or self-responsibilities to take care of at the moment.

Another thing is to realise that some of the priorities might change over time, so having a flexible approach would need to be in your thought processes as well. Try not to be too rigid in your thinking so that you can swap and change your priorities.

Balance is not better time management, but better boundary management. Balance means making choices and enjoying those choices.
Anon

It's all about a balancing act and setting priorities. Sometimes you need to have hard conversations with those around you, including your work and/or community colleagues, to express the impact accepting a position or responsibility will have on your home life. Perhaps you even suggest someone else within the group who could accept that responsibility.

Another way around this is to organise yourself. I'll refer you back to chapter four: be better organised and prioritise, get your diary up to date, make sure that your project management is good, and that you have got yourself into a good routine.

Certainly, in my re-partnered circumstances I elected not to take on the maternal role with my partner's three boys and that was set very early in our relationship.

Nigel did not want me to take on those responsibilities, but it was more my decision, because I was very strong with the fact that I had raised my two children and I did not want to take on board those responsibilities again.

When it comes to parenting, I was involved with both of my parents from a distance. My sister was the first point of contact, because she was still in Tasmania while I was in north Queensland.

I was included in a lot of the decisions that needed to be made, thanks to the sensible approach of my sister, but it also involved a lot of conversations, emotional sensitivity to my sister's and my needs to be able to make decisions that would have the best outcome.

One of the key success factors into managing the mother juggle is having a routine. Children enjoy a routine. Your

9. Managing the Mother Juggle

parents would enjoy a routine and these routines become habitual. You are then known as a reliable person in those routines and it will give you a sense of consistency in the way that you manage the household and relationships.

If you're doing things out of routine, it tends to 'upset the apple cart' and people then become a bit defensive and upset which can lead to confusion and angst.

Another aspect of managing the mother juggle is the question of your work-related responsibilities and whether you choose to be part time or full time. Sometimes there can be some flexibility in your work hours, so that when your personal responsibilities increase, you can decrease your hours. Most workplaces are quite sensible in their approach.

Consult the human resources point of contact to see if there is a way for you to perform the roles that you feel you're responsible for.

Take some time out, use your leave balances and find out whether your leave can be taken at a half rate to enable you to take your elderly parents to appointments or have the time to run the errands that might be required of you.

Likewise, with children and other responsibilities, see if you have the capacity to be flexible within your work hours. A lot of workplaces today are supportive of people working from home.

For example, if there are administrative types of activities in your work, approach your boss and explain the situation. There might be a period of weeks that you can do a proportion of your work in the home environment.

Understandably, in some professions that's not possible. Look at reducing your hours to enable you to have free time so that you don't spread yourself too thin and become stressed and unwell.

Many newer roles are 'work from home' based, and a lot of people are choosing this path to enable them to balance their home and work lives effectively.

Healthy options to take:

1. Prioritise. It's really important for you to take control of your own priorities of what you want to achieve and the input that you want to have into your immediate family and then your extended family. Recognise your value and your input to those around you. By prioritising, adding value and delegating you can free up time to put back into yourself for replenishment and refreshment.

2. Recognise your value. No one's a super mum, we're all human, so it's important that you remain humane in some of the decisions and your approaches in these situations, with or without the hormonal imbalances that are taking place.

3. Enlist your family support where you can. Your family generally can understand where you are, so by openly communicating and being a person who is transparent in what they're doing, communicating and valuing their own input, you're actually role modelling for your children more than just the practical tasks that you're teaching them.

To understand your parent's love, you must raise children yourself.
Chinese Proverb

10. Career Crossroads

Your work is going to fill a large part of your life and the only way to be truly satisfied is to do what you believe is great work. The only way to do great work is to love what you do. If you haven't found it yet, keep looking. Don't settle, as with all matters of the heart you know when you find it. And like any great relationship it just gets better and better as the years roll on. Keep looking until you find it, don't settle.
Steve Jobs

MANY OF US in our midlife years change jobs or roles due to promotion, demotion, changing tack or indeed opt for early retirement for whatever reason. It comes with mixed drivers, mixed emotions and mixed outcomes. Let's explore the journey of optional career change or choosing to stay the same.

There might be several reasons why a change is required, and it's common that people change their career paths many times throughout their career. It's very rare these days that somebody stays in the same position for their entire career. Conducting due diligence on yourself and the decisions for making the switch can save a lot of heartache, time, and ultimately, money.

Changing jobs is scary. It can be scary due to genuine fear, it can be scary due to not having the confidence in a new position learning new skills, it can be scary because of the risks that you might be taking in making the change.

Doing due diligence, understanding the pros and the cons, and the risks, makes that decision more important. If you have been made redundant or are in a situation where you have had to leave your workplace, there are professional and legal avenues that you can pursue if needed. These are beyond the scope of this book. However, it has to be recognised how stressful some of these situations are.

Why would you want to change your career path? Maybe you have an unmet need where you have not had a sense of fulfilment in your workplace and you want to find that purpose in another vocation. There might be monetary reasons, such as increasing your wage so that you can ensure that you do live your life comfortably.

During these midlife years, if you haven't planned your financial concerns in detail, then you may be entering a period of 'pre-retirement panic'.

(For more details about some financial strategies, refer to the next chapter, 'Avoiding the Financial Vacuum'.)

10. Career Crossroads

You might want to explore your fulfilment needs. If you're in a situation where this isn't possible within your work environment, then maybe another option to fulfil that gap is to find a pastime or a hobby where your sense of fulfilment can be achieved. This might be through a sporting group or a community services club, where that drive or purpose can be met.

You may not be in a situation that you can change jobs or career, therefore recognising the value that you bring to your workplace is important. We're fortunately getting into an age now where a lot of employers value the more senior workers in their environment. They understand that the value that they bring to the environment cannot be readily replaced. How wonderful!

There is a lot of investment that goes into training and upskilling, and they say it generally takes about two years for employers to get a return on their investment from training a new employee. If this is not needed and the applicant can immediately fulfil the role, then it's a win-win.

Understanding and recognising the value that you bring into your workplace is paramount to your self-confidence. This shines through in your demeanour, your approach to each task you do, and the way you organise yourself in the workplace. I'm amazed at more senior nurses that I have worked with during my career that go quietly about their work and seem to achieve so much without too much commotion.

Making the decision to change positions needs to be done on good grounds and via the correct avenues. Treating your employer with a bit of respect will allow you to leave that workplace on good terms so that you can leave the door open. The old saying, 'Don't burn your bridges' still applies, even in this fast-paced, hi-tech world.

Making the switch

There's a perception that people feel that they're too old to change jobs, and this is where due diligence and investigating all your options is paramount. Is the risk of changing the job going to give you satisfaction? Is it worth taking the risk? And are you confident enough to learn those new skills?

Going back to value, some people are fearful of changing to a new job because they think that younger people do a better job than them. This might be quite valid, so maybe a different role in the organisation would be more suitable and safer for you to work through to your desired retirement age.

Value your own input and identify education opportunities that might be available to you. If that's the pathway for you to feel fulfilled in your position, then that will enable you to stay insightful in the position that you currently have. Some people think that they're too old to learn new things; I'd like to think that you are never too old to learn something new. It might just depend on the complexities and how it's been taught to you.

In the 1950s, job security was a big issue and a lot of men stayed in their jobs for their entire career. That is one of the fear factors of changing positions or looking at other opportunities. Sometimes we do get to this age and ask ourselves whether we've fulfilled our lifetime's work and a lot of people can't or haven't identified what that looks like.

What is your lifetime's work for you to feel fulfilled?

During the midlife years, women in particular use work to supplement the family income. Years ago, women didn't go out to work, they relied on their husbands to provide the income.

10. Career Crossroads

> The overall proportion of women aged 45–54 who were employed increased from 40% in 1979 to 53% in 2004.
> **Australian Bureau of Statistics, 2006.**

Now there is more emphasis on shared household responsibilities in order for the wife of the home to maintain a career, just as much as men. In some cases, these roles are now reversed.

Throughout my career, even though I stayed within the nursing profession, I adjusted my career path based on my personal circumstances at the time. I did have big career aspirations some years ago and the opportunity for me to fulfil that changed when I made personal decisions to relocate.

Rather than looking back on that whole experience as a negative one, I saw it as an opportunity for me to grow and enrich what I was doing based on the career progression I had achieved.

For me, working as a nurse and now as a health and wellness coach, everything that I've done up until this point has led to me being a better nurse, a better whole person for me to give value back to the community to which I belong. That's all to do with my attitude.

When the opportunities changed for me I did feel very frustrated at the time, but I worked through that quite diligently using my own emotions and thoughts to stay positive. I looked at the value of what I had done and putting value on what I do every day made me recognise all the work and the study that I had done to that point was not wasted but has contributed to my development and learning.

Another thing that we need to be mindful of when making the change, whether it is a change of roles, moving to another company or changing tack, is that while we feel it might be of benefit to us and our loved ones, in fact unfortunately some work environments don't support that attitude. You can be taking a bit of a risk, and the position that you're moving to, well, the grass may not be greener on the other side.

By carrying out due diligence and identifying the aspects besides monetary reasons such as a sense of fulfilment, a sense of purpose and giving back, the decision may outweigh the negatives or the risks that you're taking.

Some people during the midlife years find that they are at an age where they prefer to work autonomously and maintain a sense of working for themselves, taking responsibility for what they're doing. There is some sense in that, but one of the common questions that I hear from my entrepreneur friends and those that work for themselves, is one vital question which is, would you employ yourself?

Do you have the work ethic to see through each day completing the tasks that you need to in order to 1) stay credible in your position 2) function with high integrity and 3) earn enough money to actually maintain the lifestyle that you enjoy, having enough income to support you independently towards retirement?

Yes, it can be daunting, it can be scary, but one of the things that I've found in developing my business 'Healthy Options Now', is that it has given me an amazing feeling of creativity and self-worth. I know that I'm developing something that is doing wonderful things for not only the clients that I serve, but the community around them.

Touching on transition to retirement

If you are in a situation where this is not required, congratulations!

If you are in employment where this may be an option, go and have a discussion with your human resources department. Some organisations now offer an early retirement program where you can bring forward your superannuation to fund the decreasing hours that you want to work.

> **Healthy options to take:**
> 1. Examine the reasons why you want to either stay in your current position or change.
> 2. Conduct the due diligence on the changes. Does it match all your goals in the longer term, including inner fulfilment? If not, can your fulfilment be met outside of the work environment?
> 3. Recognise the value you bring to the workplace.
> 4. Is transition to retirement an option? Seek human resources advice.

Do the due diligence that is required. Weigh up the pros and cons to help you make the decisions that you need to move forward in your life, so that you can enjoy the next ten to fifteen years of your working life knowing that you have done everything that you can to make it enjoyable, viable and financially rewarding for you.

11. Avoiding the Financial Vacuum

> *Forty-eight percent of Australians say they do not budget for their day to day expenses.*
> Paul Clitheroe

THIS CHAPTER IS AIMED at the average working-class midlifer who is close to paying off their mortgage, in a stable job (either self-employed or have a position with an employer) and looking at a moderate level of retirement. We're going to explore the concepts of trying to stop yourself from dwindling down that vacuum and running out of money to make sure that you have a sustainable slush fund into the future.

For those who have managed financial freedom at this age, I congratulate you, you can skip this chapter! Just make sure that you spend or invest your money wisely.

A disclaimer: I would thoroughly recommend seeing a trusted financial advisor for the exact details of your financial position.

Managing your finances really is a complex issue and the purpose of this chapter is to just give you a few tips about what you can look at to move you forward. During a lifetime you have a number of priorities that take place and the older you get, the more you want to be in a position where you can cater for those sudden, incidental expenses or the emergencies that pop up.

Do you feel confident about your financial future? What are some of your concerns about money towards retirement and beyond?

One of the things that money does give you is a sense of confidence about yourself and where you're heading. We should be at an age now where we don't need to worry about the next decision regarding financial matters. We should really be in a position where we have a buffer to manage situations where we need to fork out for medium sized purchases without too much of a ding in our financial accounts.

Don't worry, be happy!

Some of the benefits of being in a good position regarding your financial future is that you have a level of confidence. You'll be able to identify the pitfalls of bad money decisions and making informed decisions about your future. You will by this age value your attitude towards money and identify where your money is going with the use of money trackers. You'll understand lifestyle choices versus financial planning and understand how financial concerns can manifest themselves in stress, which can also then manifest themselves in problems for your health and ultimately your weight management.

11. Avoiding the Financial Vacuum

> Money isn't the most important thing in life, but it's reasonably close to oxygen on the 'gotta have it' scale.
> Zig Ziglar

Money matters: some key tips

One key tip at this age is to make sure that you have your own financial situation in place and in control prior to helping any family members. All too often I speak to clients about issues regarding their health and it is finances that come up. It's usually their worry because they've helped their loved ones or a son or a daughter to enable them to get ahead, but they don't realise that they're compromising their own financial future.

This is where a professional financial advisor can come into play and maybe tweak some of your situation, so that you aren't financially compromised for the long term.

The second thing is to make sure that you pay off any personal debt, starting with the largest percentage debt first, down to the smallest. It amazes me that some people just do not understand interest rates, and how this can blow out. Shop around for a zero-interest credit card and have the balance transferred onto that. The key thing with this is to make sure that you pay off your interest-free credit card while not using it at all.

Personal debt comes from habitual spending, and of course the whole scenario can head towards disaster. Some believe that there can be an addiction to spending. Getting that instant gratification. If that's your case, then I would recommend that you do seek professional help.

> *Beware the little expenses, a small leak will sink a great ship.*
> Benjamin Franklin

The third key thing is to know about your superannuation and the projections for it. Understand where it's going to fit in with your longer-term plans. I am surprised when I hear midlifers taking their superannuation money as an interim measure prior to taking the aged pension. How many times do we hear mortgage lenders who seem to calculate your borrowing capacity well beyond your retirement age? Are they are considering that you will possibly use your superannuation to pay back your mortgage?

Sure, the reasons for this may be varied: to pay off other loans, to re-invest (a gamble I say), or again to help a family member. My message is to look after yourself first.

Fundamental to all of this is to understand your financial situation as it is today. Money mapping is a great activity to undertake. Keep your own accounts, either on an app, on a computer or on paper and identify where your money's being spent.

A lot of people when doing an activity like this become shocked by the wasteful spending. The 'one coffee a day' habit can buy you a new refrigerator at the end of the year. A lot of people can't compute that a daily habit can have that outcome at the end of 12 months.

Think about your finances in a 12-month cycle; rather than thinking about living from week to week, work it out year to year, so that you know exactly at what months of the year you're going to have an increase in bills and budget for those bills.

11. Avoiding the Financial Vacuum

Also, set up your accounts to pay bills as your pay comes in, if you're in a situation to be able to do that and not actually count money and budget money for bills and lifestyle. A lot of people do their budget so that two thirds of their income goes towards expenses with a third going towards lifestyle and day to day expenses.

I think the most important thing about being a midlifer is to value what you're putting into the household and to make sure that you are rewarding yourself for your financial health.

During my lifetime, I have owned a house, divorced, re-established myself and then partnered again. Throughout all those changes has been the financial component, but what's been most important for me to rationalise is the health and wellbeing of myself and my family as they take priority. Realistically, although I'm in a good position now, 15 years ago when I was heading into those difficult times, I couldn't really forecast my vision of being in a position to retire comfortably in the future.

A lot of my clients feel that they don't have the capacity to earn enough for the lifestyle that they dream of after their retirement. This lures some people down a path where they're taking risks, gambling their financial situation in order to achieve the lifestyle that they want to achieve towards the end of their life. This is a highly vulnerable age where stress and anxiety can take over because of financial concerns.

The key thing there with any thoughts about changing your position for financial gain is to make sure that you are doing your due diligence. Seek advice from someone in the field that you trust and know or have known for quite some time, so that you are guided towards a sensible decision.

> **Healthy options to take:**
> 1. Look after your own finances first.
> 2. Pay off any personal debt as a priority.
> 3. Set realistic lifestyle goals heading into retirement.
> 4. Seek trusted financial advice where necessary.

12. You Did It!

Now I can wear heels!
Nicole Kidman (on divorcing Tom Cruise)

YOU ABSOLUTELY DID IT! If not all of it, some part of it. You're gaining momentum and steaming forward. Congratulations! All too often we achieve things and we do not take the time out to celebrate our successes.

This chapter is all about celebration and staying on track.

A lot of people are modest about their successes and celebration of success often gets pushed to one side. If you've worked so hard to achieve success in maintaining a certain goal weight, all too often we just switch back into our day to day routine. The success that you've achieved doesn't get acknowledged by the most important person: that's you.

By celebrating success, you build on your self-esteem and confidence, recognise where you come from and can see where you are going. Looking back and reflecting, you can acknowledge the achievement that you have made.

The key here is that if you do have a setback, you understand those setbacks and identify where you can return to these strategies or put yourself back on track to stay on target.

> *Failure is an important part of your growth and developing resilience. Don't be afraid to fail.*
> **Michelle Obama**

Set yourself realistic celebratory moments. As I said at the beginning in chapter two, it's a really good idea to set yourself smaller goals more often, so that when you achieve those goals, you give yourself a bit of time out to go and do something that is a reward for you. By reward, we're talking about something that is positive and enhances your lifestyle.

Some examples of rewards could be to go and get a massage, buy a new outfit or part of a new outfit, a piece of jewellery, or have a nice meal out with those that you love. When you achieve a major success for a major goal, that's where you could invest more time and money and celebrate the success.

Others around you will notice your increased confidence and self-esteem, and that comes back to you. They do say that what you put out into the universe comes back to you tenfold and I believe that to be true.

Over the period of time of you incorporating these strategies, you would have identified strategies of your own that have worked really well. It's important during your reflection and journaling process to pull out those strategies again, revisit how they felt, think about what actually happened, and really explore and research those strategies.

What celebration does to your body:

It gives you positive feedback through all those happy hormones; you're feeding back those positive vibes in the brain system to identify and enhance physical outcomes. The enjoyment hormones and neurones give you a sense of satisfaction. Use incremental celebrations as stepping stones; think of it as going across the river where you've got the stepping stones to get to the other side of the beautiful waterfall.

Using those stepping stones time and time again will help you get there.

Recognise the celebratory moments. If people around you are paying you a compliment, then really take it on board, soak it up like a sponge, really enjoy the moment that they're giving you when they've acknowledged the difference in you.

Document your success too. Use photos or videos – look back on incidental photos and videos. You know yourself when you look at somebody who's beaming in a photo where the expression on their face and their body language is extremely positive, you can tell when they are in a happy place.

Write stories if you're a writer. Journaling, documenting and writing them down will be helpful to you and if you are a diary keeper or journal writer, keep on doing it, you will have such a wealth of stories and affirmations to use later.

Some people use things like a dot journal, make picture diagrams, drawings or calligraphy. That whole process of self-expression written down in a book can be a great reminder of where you've come from.

Keep all your certifications; if as a result of these lifestyle changes you've actually achieved an academic qualification or been awarded at the pinnacle of your sports club, keep those certificates in a prominent visual place in your home to remind you of your achievements and give you a sense of satisfaction that you've achieved those goals.

There is a reason why people keep a 'pool room', that is so they can go back into those rooms and look around them and see those moments in time where they did achieve successes, filling up their bank of feeling positive about themselves.

When you're looking back on the 12 months, depending on the timeframe is that it's taken you to achieve these lifestyle changes, writing in your journal you can decide if you want to take it that one step further and pull out your own system for staying on track. The beauty of this is that you can repeat those systems or the steps year after year and stay focussed on achieving a goal every 12 months.

It's really a good idea to set up a goal at the end of the 12 months so that once you've achieved 80% of what the goal is and above, you can go ahead and perform the rest.

Using positive affirmations are extremely powerful, so build yourself up with words such as 'I can change', 'I do support myself', 'I am resilient', 'I make good choices' and 'I have good strengths'. These are just a few examples of how you can speak to yourself and build your self-esteem.

Following my divorce in 2005, and after having undergone the transformation of losing weight in my forties, I'd always dreamed of being able to travel internationally. That dream became a reality in 2010 through my work and capitalising on an opportunity that came to me. I was successfully awarded a scholarship to study at the Royal Marsden in London. I took some long service leave and I expanded it and ended

12. You Did It!

up doing a wonderful trip to Scotland and Europe. I made some amazing friends who I'm still in close contact with, but that was a lifetime dream that I never thought I'd be able to experience. When I was under the blanket of maintaining a household and family, and going through those experiences, it felt that blanket had lifted, and I was able to be set free.

There was a sense of pride on being able to achieve that, so much so that I've got a spread of photos on a board in my family room. Every day I look at that board and it takes me back to all the places that we visited and all the experiences that we had, and more importantly, the feeling of positivity that that experience gave me. To me that was the pinnacle of what I had set out to achieve in losing all my weight in my forties.

More recently, my fiftieth birthday weekend was two years ago. I pulled together those nearest and dearest to me and had a wonderful weekend away with them in a hinterland lodge.

It was because my birthday is during winter, and in southeast Queensland you actually need to get to elevation to get those nice cold temperatures. It revisited in my own mind, my childhood upbringing around the fire and having that sense of family and those ones close to you. I had that for three days with my family, and it was just beautiful.

That was really a celebration of a major milestone in my life for my fiftieth birthday, but it was also a milestone that I had re-partnered; I felt that I had nurtured my family and taken them through those years of working it out following divorce.

It's paramount that you celebrate those major milestones in a significant way that pulls together your heartstrings, that makes an impact on how you feel and how you think.

Once again, congratulations, I hope that you have put into action some of the suggestions in this book and have achieved your goals. Now that you've tackled the lifestyle changes that you wanted to make, your journey is now ongoing.

Celebrate your life, celebrate your achievements, and be proud of who you are.

Family, nature and health all go together.
Olivia Newton John

About the Author

By Jodie Marsh
Clinical Nurse Specialist, Townsville

I first met Wendy almost twenty years ago. I was a young unmarried twenty-something junior staff nurse and Wendy was a married thirty-something Nurse Educator. At that point in her life, Wendy never seemed to be truly happy. At thirty, she seemed older than her biological age.

Over the past twenty years I watched as Wendy went through a divorce, moved to a new town, changed her career path and successfully raised two well-adjusted children. As she progressed though all these changes I witnessed Wendy successfully commence a life journey to fitness and health – not only physically but on a mental and spiritual level also.

Wendy was always a smart, strong woman but along the way she has changed not only her physical being but also her outlook on life. Her journey to this is inspiring – so much so that at 39 I decided that I did not want to be fat at forty. If Wendy could change herself in her forties why couldn't I do it in my thirties? By the time I turned forty, I had lost 20 kg and have since continued my path to fitness and health. Over the years, Wendy has encouraged me in my career, inspired me in life and continued to prove that if you have the drive, age is no barrier to achieving any goals that you set for yourself regardless of the challenges that life throws at you or the ups and downs that you may face.

When I look at Wendy now, I see the fifty-something that could be thirty-something. Through her own determination she has made herself happy. She is proof that if you put yourself in the right headspace you can not only inspire yourself but take others on the journey with you. Wendy is truly a role model for how to live your life happily and healthily.

Speaker Profile

Wendy Trevarthen is a qualified Health and Wellness Coach, an experienced Registered Nurse, a Personal Trainer, as well as a mother, grandmother, partner and mentor to many. She has been involved in healthcare all her career and has seen firsthand the dramatic effects of chronic illness, not only on the patient but the extended family members.

Awarded with two Queensland Cancer Council Awards in her career, including study at the Royal Marsden Hospital in London, Wendy has extensively applied her knowledge and skills. As a Nurse Educator, and Clinical Facilitator she has imparted her knowledge to student nurses, post-graduate nurses, and colleagues.

Combining her personal journey with professional experience spanning three decades, she has put together her signature 12-month program which this book outlines.

As a wellness advocate her vision is to enable midlifers to live the life they deserve by implementing easy strategies for sustainable lifestyle options.

Speaker Profile

Wendy can speak on the following:

- Finding your MidLife Mojo
    - Your unique 12-month blueprint
    - Develop a successful mind-set
    - Aging with dignity and poise
- Creating healthy habits
    - Tasty food swaps that stick
    - Create an exercise habit
    - Beat procrastination
    - 'Rev that engine'
    - Bust your midlife clutter
- Learning about pre-disease
    - Signs and symptoms - What do they all mean?
    - Incorporating lifestyle around pre-disease
    - Managing the family domino effect

Contact details:
- Mobile 0457 833 009
- www.healthyoptionsnow.org
- wendy@healthyoptionsnow.org

Packages

What's included	MidLife Mojo Workshop	Eight Weeks to Healthy Habits	Find Your MidLife Mojo
MidLife Mojo: You're 50, Cut the Crap…	X	X	X
Membership to social media groups	X	X	X
Five-day challenges	X	X	X
Twelve-month workbook	X		X
Develop an exercise habit that sticks		X	X
Healthy food swaps that satisfy		X	X
Eight weeks to rev your engine again		X	X
Beat procrastination		X	X
Clutter buster program		X	X
One-hour personal goal setting session			X
Ten 1-hour group sessions over 12 months			X
Twelve-month diary			X
CSIRO Wellbeing Diet Resource Book			X
Fortnightly online updates			X
Exercise modification video series			X
Membership to VIP club			X

Note: Nurses receive 10% discount on programs.
Corporate enquiries welcome.

www.ingramcontent.com/pod-product-compliance
Lightning Source LLC
Chambersburg PA
CBHW030041100526
44590CB00011B/287